The Parables Of Jesus

Applications For Contemporary Life

Cycle A

Richard Gribble

CSS Publishing Company, Inc., Lima, Ohio

THE PARABLES OF JESUS, CYCLE A

Copyright © 1998 by
CSS Publishing Company, Inc.
Lima, Ohio

Scripture quotations are from the *New Revised Standard Version of the Bible*, copyright 1989 by the Division of Christian Education of the National Council of the Churches of Christ in the USA. Used by permission.

Paraphrased stories from John Aurelio, *Colors! Stories of the Kingdom* © 1993, used with permission of The Crossroad Publishing Company, New York.

Paraphrase of "Lily" from Walter Wangerin, Jr., *Ragman And Other Cries of Faith* © 1984, used with permission of HarperCollins Publishers, New York.

Library of Congress Cataloging-in-Publication Data

Gribble, Richard.
    The parables of Jesus : applications for contemporary life, Cycle A / Richard Gribble.
        p.   cm.
    Includes bibliographical references.
    ISBN 0-7880-1197-9
    1. Jesus Christ—Parables—Sermons.   2. Sermons, American.   I. Title.
BT375.2.G73   1998
251'.6—DC21
                                                                                98-5191
                                                                                CIP

This book is available in the following formats, listed by ISBN:
        0-7880-1197-9   Book
        0-7880-1198-7   IBM
        0-7880-1199-5   MAC
        0-7880-1200-2   Sermon Prep

PRINTED IN U.S.A.

Dedication

Inspiration comes in various forms and degrees. While the ideas that are contained in this volume were inspired by my desire to preach God's word in the parish, this book would never have been written without the support and care that must accompany any significant endeavor. This book is dedicated to my many friends who have supported me and whose lives of faith illustrate the love of God to me.

Preface

For almost two thousand years the Christian community throughout the world has assembled each Sunday to praise God. Gathered on the Lord's Day, the day of Christ's triumphal resurrection, Christians celebrate in word and sacrament the presence of God in our world, both our individual lives and human society collectively. While celebration of the Eucharist is a common practice for all Christian denominations, the word of God transmitted to us in Sacred Scripture is universally held to be central to worship. The Bible challenges and inspires us; it reveals the message of God and provides a road map for the faithful to follow as they daily travel the path that leads to God and eternal life.

While each individual finds a special pearl in the vast treasure of Scripture, most people agree that the Gospels present the heart of Jesus' message. Written by people of faith at different times and for varied audiences, the Gospels provide accounts of the words and deeds of Jesus Christ from his birth, through his public ministry in Israel, and culminating in his passion, death, and resurrection. The evangelists' accounts vary, but the core of Christ's teaching — faith, love of God and neighbor, forgiveness and reconciliation, and service — echoes through all four Gospels. These books of the Bible are familiar to all Christians, who are schooled in them from childhood. Each Sunday service or Mass contains a reading from one of the Gospels.

The best known literary form presented in the Gospels is the parable. Many of the parables have become Bible favorites because of their familiar, appealing, and challenging teachings. The parables of the prodigal son (Luke 15:1-32), the sower (Matthew 13:1-9, 18-23), the uncaring judge (Luke 18:1-8), the Good Shepherd (John 10:11-18), and the Good Samaritan (Luke 10:25-37) are known and quoted by Christians throughout the world.

Jesus used parables to enter into dialogue with his disciples and opponents alike. By their nature parables present their message in an indirect manner; their meaning is not obvious, but open to interpretation. Reading the parables with the eyes of Christians approaching the third millennium, we will most probably obtain an understanding different than that of the first hearers of Jesus' words.

In order for the parable to maintain the timelessness of Scripture, the message contained in the story must be applied to our contemporary environment and culture. It is the awesome task of the preacher to make the Scriptures come alive for the faithful who worship in our churches. This book is my effort to apply the Gospel message to today's world with all its beauty, difficulties, and challenges.

Preachers and those wishing to understand the parables better can use this volume to open new doors of insight into the infinite treasure of Christ's message to the world. This book presents a theme and spiritual food for our daily journey, applying the parable's message in a contemporary context. Sample sermon openings together with questions for reflection and challenge provide preachers with one possible road map in preparing a sermon. Lastly, each parable is analyzed through exegesis and is placed in context within the liturgical year, with the other Gospels, and the two additional Scripture lessons of the day.

This book is a combination of personal reflection, prayer, and research. As many scholars have discovered various meanings in the parables, so preachers will differ in their method of applying these powerful stories to today's world. It is my hope that the reader will find my reflections and ideas a challenge. If preachers are not challenged, if they cannot convince themselves of the importance and contemporary viability of the message of Scripture, they will never win over those who hear God's word and seek guidance in its application. The messages of the parables outlined in this book speak to me of the need for God. May those who use this volume experience that same need.

Richard Gribble, CSC

Table Of Contents

Introduction

Gospel, Parable, And The Matthean Tradition

The parables of Jesus are possibly the best known sections of Sacred Scripture. Reading the Gospels, it is impossible to proceed far without encountering one of the many accounts that have been classified by scholars and novices alike as parables. Christians have been schooled from childhood on the important messages and teachings related by the four Gospel evangelists that have been transmitted as stories told by Jesus to his disciples and opponents. In order to understand more completely the message and significance of Jesus' words it is important to gain some insight into the literary form of gospel where parables were used and what precisely is meant by the concept of parable. The fact that the synoptic authors and John use parables in different ways also necessitates an understanding of the tradition of the evangelists, their sources, audience, and purpose of composition. This chapter serves to introduce the reader to the concepts of gospel and parable and how they are utilized in the work of Saint Matthew.

The Gospel Tradition

The word "gospel" finds its roots in the Greek *euangelion,* meaning the good news. For the people of the early church *euangelion* signified not a book that chronicled and emphasized the significance of Jesus' words and actions, but rather the good news of Messianic salvation present in Christ's life. Such good tidings were first proclaimed by the Prophet Isaiah (52:7): "How beautiful upon the mountains are the feet of the messenger who announces peace, who brings good news, who announces salvation, who says to Zion, 'Your God reigns.' " Jesus preached the good news (Mark 1:15, Matthew 11:5, and Luke 4:18) to all who would listen. The good news was also found in the apostolic preaching concerning Christ and the salvation that is found in him (Acts 5:42 and Romans 1:1ff).

The Gospels were not the original source of information about Jesus and his message of salvation; the Gospels were not written by Jesus. They are accounts of Christ's words and deeds as they were remembered by others. The writings of the evangelists may be precisely what Jesus said and did, but it is much more likely that the accuracy we assume in contemporary historical writing is not present here. This should not be disturbing for several reasons. First, since there are four different Gospel accounts of Jesus' activities, written at different times for various reasons, it would be virtually impossible for total agreement in dates, times, and specific actions. This is clearly evident when one compares the synoptic accounts with each other and especially with John. The Gospels were not all (possibly none) written by eyewitnesses to the events related; the authors, therefore, used sources to generate their works. Oral tradition and written sources were combined with the opinion and agenda of the writer to produce accounts which portray the purpose and message of Jesus in a particular light.

The Gospels are not biographies of Jesus nor are they accurate historical documents. The evangelists did not try to relate everything that Jesus did (John 21:25). Rather, they selected material from sources available to fashion a written account of Christ's life that would be understandable to readers, transmit the message of salvation, and portray Jesus as he was perceived by the writer. The Gospels were not written to be accurate histories; they are writings of faith. One need look no further than the difference between the synoptics and John on the length of Jesus' public ministry (one year versus three) to realize the lack of historicity in the texts. The objective of the evangelists in general was to demonstrate the ministry of the Messiah from its favorable beginning in Galilee, to its tragic conclusion in Jerusalem, and its ultimate triumph through resurrection. Modern historic writing demands a detailed and accurate chronology, but the lack of historical accuracy in the Gospels does not defeat the writer's purpose nor deflate the importance of Christ's ministry.

The Gospels were written many years after the events they describe, using sources available to the evangelists. Mark, judged today by scholars as the first Gospel written, used literary works, including the Roman catechesis of Peter, and oral tradition as its principal sources. Matthew and Luke used Mark, supplementing it with a common Q (German *Quelle*) source and material particular to each writer. John, standing apart from the synoptic tradition, produced a very different account. Some scholars suggest he wrote to supplement the synoptics and others believe that he wrote a completely different account with no knowledge of the accounts of Matthew, Mark, and Luke. Close similarities in all accounts of the crucifixion, however, indicate that this was a well-known event in the apostolic age and that it had been communicated in a consistent manner in oral and written sources.

The Synoptic Gospels all follow a basic format. The first part of each account describes Jesus' preparation for his public ministry and his baptism by John. Next, the evangelists describe in various forms of detail the ministry of Jesus in Galilee. The Messiah's journey with his disciples from Galilee to Jerusalem, complete with predictions of Jesus' death, is then related. All three evangelists conclude their accounts in Jerusalem with a chronicle of the passion, death, and resurrection of the Lord. The aforementioned similarity of the passion narratives tells scholars that this section of these Gospels was probably written first.

Those familiar with Sacred Scripture are well aware that there are many other writings of the period that are not part of the Canon. This fact raises the question of how the canon was produced and what criteria were used in its selection. Four basic criteria were used to determine the canonical status of the many sacred writings. Apostolic origin was the first criterion. Authorship by one of the chosen twelve or those known as apostles in the early church gave immediate credibility to any writing. Next, those charged with developing the canon looked at the community addressed in writings. This criterion was especially applicable in the Pauline corpus and other writings ascribed to Paul. Conformity to the rule of faith was a third criterion. A document may have been attributed to an apostle, but if its content was inconsistent with the message of salvation as understood by the people of the day, then its validity was highly suspect and importance suppressed. Lastly, as a review of the volumes of apocrypha and pseudepigrapha reveals, there are numerous writings that seem to fit the basic criteria set for acceptability, yet they are not part of the canon of Scripture. Thus, the element of chance in the final selection must not be discounted.

Parable In Concept And Use

In order to describe the purpose and meaning of Jesus' words which we know as parable, some basic understanding of this term must be given. One definition suitable for our purposes is: "Every parable is a story; this story conveys a lesson so that the parable has a double meaning, the story and the lesson; the parable's purpose is to effect a change in the hearer, to lead to decision or action; and the lesson always is religious or moral."[1] In modern usage the term parable should be and usually is reserved for those stories which are drawn from ordinary everyday life, which have a religious or moral lesson conveyed indirectly, and which are intended to convince or persuade and to bring the hearer to decision or action.

Each parable has four distinct elements. First, parables are narratives which tell stories, generally of a popular or folk nature. These stories are told, however, on two levels, the literal and the topical. Parabolic stories convey a message that is indirect, often only implicit. Thirdly, parables are far more than entertainment; they are told to bring about a change of mind or even better a change of heart (the Greek *metanoia*) in the hearer. The call to conversion is also heard in these message-laden stories. Hearers of the parable cannot be neutral; they must accept or reject the lesson. In this sense parables are rhetorical. Lastly, parables, in conveying a religious or ethical message, also present a challenge in living the interrelationship between the human and the divine.

Literary criticism demonstrates the similarities and differences between parable and allegory. In a parable one single point of comparison is presented; the details of the story have no independent significance. This last idea distinguishes parable from allegory, for in the latter each detail has a symbolic significance. This distinction should not be presented too rigorously, however, for it is not uncommon, especially in an extended parable, that certain details are inserted precisely because they suit the intended application. A rigid distinction is also unwise when one sees that the concept of parable in Scripture is broad, like the Hebrew concept of *mashal*, a term that includes figurative speech of every kind.

Three basic forms of parable are found in the Gospels. Similitude, the most concise form, tells a typical or recurrent event from real life that would be familiar to all hearers. The similitude gains its persuasiveness by recounting what is widely recognized as true. Examples of this form include the parables of the lost coin (Luke 15:8-10) and the growing seed (Mark 4:26-29). The form labeled "parable" is often (though not always) longer and more detailed than the similitude. This literary genre tells a story, not about something recurrent in real life, but about a one-time event which is fictitious. Although they are fables, parables never indulge the fanciful or fantastic; they remain true to life. Usually narrated in the past tense, parables derive their cogency from the single, vivid, and fresh way they engage the hearer. Numerous synoptic parables use this form, including the stories of the persistent widow (Luke 18:1-8) and the two sons (Matthew 21:28-30). Exemplary story is the third form of Gospel parable. Like the other two forms, exemplary story presents an implied comparison between an event drawn from real life and the reality of the moral or religious order. Rather than drawing a distinction between two very different things (as do similitude and parable), the exemplary story presents a single example, one specific case, which illustrates a general principle. Luke's Gospel contains all four exemplary stories — the Good Samaritan (10:29-37), the rich fool (12:16-21), the rich man and Lazarus (16:19-31), and the Pharisee and tax collector (18:9-14).

The timelessness of the gospel message is present in the way parables serve their twofold purpose to present a story with a lesson. Parables derive their material from real life, from the everyday world of family and friends, work and worship. They are always drawn from the experiences of Jesus and his audience. For the most part the parables are set in the rural life of Israel. Though the setting is contemporary and common, the experiences that are narrated transcend that time and place; they speak to hearers of all ages and cultures. Although the material is drawn from everyday life, some parables have elements which move from the ordinary to the extraordinary, such as the yeast as leaven (Matthew 13:33 and Luke 13:20-21) or the unforgiving servant (Matthew 18:23-35). These features demonstrate that parables deal with matters transcending ordinary life.

The concept of parable, although most common to us in the Gospels, has deep roots in the Mediterranean world where it was used as a teaching technique. In Greece and Rome parables were employed by rhetoricians, politicians, and philosophers, including Socrates and Aristotle. In Israel parables were used by the Old Testament prophets as well as Jewish rabbis who were contemporaries of Jesus. In the Gospels a parable may be a proverb, such as "Doctor, cure yourself" (Luke 4:23), as well as its more common use as story and lesson.

Any discussion of the parables must ask what Jesus' purpose was in using this indirect method to proclaim his message. Scholars today generally agree that Christ did not use parables primarily to convey general religion and ethical truths or as weapons of warfare for defense or attack. Thus, Jesus did not use parables to convey information or enter into debate. Rather, Christ used them to win his audience to his view; they became instruments of dialogue between Jesus and his audience. The Lord's aim was to engage his hearers' attention and to gain their assent in order that they could adopt his views. Indeed, Jesus used parables as a means of dialogue where he presented his views and perceptions and anticipated the objections of his listeners. The parable became the primary vehicle whereby Jesus taught both his disciples and his opponents.

Why did Jesus teach some of his most important lessons using parables? Mark 4:10-12 suggests that he wanted to conceal his teachings from those outside the immediate fold: "When he was alone, those who were around him along with the twelve asked him about the parables. And he said to them, 'To you has been given the secret of the kingdom of God, but for those outside, everything comes in parables; in order that they may indeed look,

14

but not perceive, and may indeed listen, but not understand; so that they may not turn again and be forgiven.' " Scholars have wrestled with these verses, perceiving them to be contradictory to Jesus' need to teach all people. However, it is probable that Christ would use parables to conceal his teaching and make it more difficult for those who sought to find fault and accuse him of sedition. Additional reasons to use parables were to reveal and illustrate his message to his disciples and as a tool to disarm his listeners. At times Jesus sought to penetrate the hostility and hardness of heart of his listeners by means of a parable.

The Tradition Of Matthew

Tradition says that the author of the Gospel of Matthew was the tax collector Jesus called to be his follower in the Galilean ministry. The earliest witness to Matthean authorship is found in Papias, Bishop of Hierapolis (130 AD) in Asia Minor. Although Papias' five-volume work *Explanation of the Lord's Sayings*, which credits Matthew as the author of the Gospel, is not extant, Eusebius (260-339) in his *Church History* quotes from the work. Irenaeus and Origen also testify to Matthean authorship.

Contemporary scholarship challenges the traditional view that the apostle Matthew penned the Gospel that bears his name. The work's dependence upon outside sources leads exegetes today to conclude that the work could not have been written by an immediate disciple of Jesus. The "Two-Source Theory" has been used to explain Matthew's use of Mark and "Q" as the principal sources for his account. The author's dependence on Mark and its prediction of the destruction of Jerusalem (24:15-20) make it certain that the Gospel was written sometime after 70 AD (the date of the Temple's destruction by the Romans). Several scholars suggest a date of 85-90 AD because many of the theological concerns and perspectives of the Gospel are those of a "second generation" Christian. Such a late date would almost preclude Matthean authorship, as the apostle would most probably have been dead by this time.

The place of origin of Matthew's Gospel is also uncertain, but tradition gives Antioch as the city of composition. The Gospel's deep concern with the relations between the church and Judaism suggests that it must have been written in an area where Christianity and Judaism were in continual contact and conflict and where Jewish influence was sufficiently strong to bring serious trouble to the communities of Christian believers. Antioch, where the Gospel message was first proclaimed to Gentiles and where the disciples were first called Christians (Acts 11:26), fits this description. The extraordinary influence that this Gospel achieved within a few decades leads scholars to believe it must have been sponsored by an exceptionally important Christian community, such as Antioch. Antioch inaugurated the missionary journey of Paul and Barnabas (Acts 13:1-3) and was visited by Peter (Galatians 2:11ff). The distinct probability that the Gospel was originally written in Aramaic for Jewish-Christians, then promptly translated into Greek (the form we have), gives more evidence for Antioch since many Jewish converts in Antioch, through the influence of Hellenization, spoke Greek. While other cities were favorable to Christianity, there is no significant reason why the tradition of Antioch as the place of origin cannot stand today.

The Gospel of Matthew has been described as a manual of instruction in the Christian way of life which the author sees as the fulfillment in Jesus Christ of the revelation of God given to Israel and preserved in Scripture. This instruction, centered around Jesus who by word and deed has inaugurated the kingdom of heaven, is structured in a series of narratives and discourses bracketed by accounts of the birth and infancy of Jesus and his passion, death, and resurrection. The bulk of the Gospel contains five sections, each consisting of a narrative followed by a discourse. In the five sections the evangelist uses his principal theological construct of the kingdom of heaven, describing its promulgation (chapters 3-7), preaching (chapters 8-10), mystery (chapters 11-13), relation to the church (chapters 13-18), and near advent (chapters 19-25).

The Gospels, because they report most directly the message and actions of Jesus, hold a special place in Sacred Scripture. Writing to various peoples at different times and for specific reasons, the evangelists composed accounts that differ in content, structure, theme, and emphasis. In the synoptic accounts of Matthew, Mark, and Luke the use of parable is one important unifying thread.

As we will see, several parables are found in various forms that provide different messages to readers, depending on the evangelist's need to present certain teachings of Jesus. The varied accounts of the Gospels provide a rich treasure that can be explored by contemporary readers as they daily search for the meaning of Christ's words and teachings in their lives. Applying the parables to contemporary life is a challenge faced by all who read and preach the gospel. The timelessness of Jesus' message tells us that meaning can be found; it is our task to discover it.

---

1. Madeleine I. Boucher, *The Parables*, Revised Edition (Wilmington, Delaware; Michael Glazier, Inc., 1983), p. 19.

Chapter 1

Illuminating God's Message To The World

Matthew 5:13-16

"You are the salt of the earth; but if salt has lost its taste, how can its saltiness be restored? It is no longer good for anything, but it is thrown out and trampled under foot.
"You are the light of the world. A city built on a hill cannot be hid. No one after lighting a lamp puts it under a bushel basket, but on the lampstand, and it gives light to all in the house. In the same way, let your light shine before others, so that they may see your good works and give glory to your Father in heaven."

Theme

Images of salt and light hold center stage in this short pericope at the outset of the Sermon on the Mount. The parable expresses in general the need for Jesus' apostles, and by extension all his followers, to live lives which enhance society, as salt gives flavor to food, and to illumine the world with the teachings of Christ, as a light brightens a darkened room. Today our world suffers from personal and communal sin which makes society unappealing and uninviting to the Christian. Society also suffers from the darkness of ignorance that obscures the teachings of Christ. Discipleship requires that we "salt" our world with Jesus' message and illumine it with God's presence, acting as evangelists in all that we do and say.

Spiritual Food For The Journey

It is not easy to be a Christian in our world, but then Jesus never promised that being a disciple would be easy. In fact, the Lord promised the opposite. To be salt of the earth and light of the world is a great challenge indeed. To salt the earth and preserve it from corruption requires our action. To illumine Christ to the world we must respond to his challenge to be disciples. In general the Lord asks us to be responsible people, lead holy lives, and help him in building the kingdom in our day.

Our task of being salt and light requires in general that we be Christ to one another. Saint Teresa of Avila, a sixteenth-century mystic and religious reformer, once wrote a prayer which beautifully describes our task:

> *Christ has no hands but yours — no hands or feet but yours. Yours are the eyes through which Christ looks with compassion on the world. Christ has no hands but yours.*

May we believe and profess the same.

Application Of The Parable To Contemporary Life

Sermon Openings
1. In his inaugural address on January 20, 1961, President John F. Kennedy proclaimed, "Ask not what your country can do for you; ask what you can do for your country." Kennedy's words challenged Americans to reflect on their response to a nation, the United States of America, which has provided so much for so many people. From its inception, our nation is one which has been called a land of promise. It is a nation where human rights, freedom, and a democratic form of government are protected by the Constitution. It is a land of opportunity where all people, at least in theory, can participate. It is a country where we can drive our own car, buy our own home, and work wherever we choose.

What has been the reaction of Americans to this land of plenty and opportunity? For some the response has been to answer the call to arms in time of war. For another generation it was a call to unity, sacrifice, and change as the nation fought to escape the pit of the Great Depression. For others the response to America has been one of defiance to authority and structure. Some have responded with violence and still others have perceived themselves unaccountable in such recent events as Watergate and the Iran-Contra affair.

The parables of salt and light call us to witness and to respond to God. As John F. Kennedy called the American people to accountability, so Jesus asks us to reflect on how we can be salt for the earth and make efforts to illumine our world with God's message of peace and love. Being salt and light might cost us something; we may have to take a chance. But then, how often has God gone out on a limb for us, through the gifts of free will, the ability to think, and the opportunity to say yes or no to the Lord each day?

2. On the battlefield a chaplain encountered a wounded soldier lying in pain in a foxhole. "Would you like me to read to you from this good book, the Bible?" The man could only respond, "I'm so thirsty." The chaplain dutifully ran off, found a canteen, and poured the soldier a drink of water. The wounded man was shifting around as if he were very uncomfortable. Thus, the chaplain found a bed roll and placed it under the man's head as a pillow. The soldier then began to shiver. Without thinking the chaplain stripped off his own field jacket and laid it over the wounded man. The soldier then looked the chaplain in the eye and said, "Now if there is anything in that book of yours that will allow a man to do more for another than you have already done, then please read it, because I would like to hear it."

Three students were discussing various versions of the Bible. One said, "I like the *New American Bible*. It is easier to read than the older versions." A second student commented, "I like the *Jerusalem Bible*. It too is easier to read and it is poetic in its style. I can use it in my daily prayer." The third student stood and said,

"I like my mother's version the best. She translated the Bible into action so I can use it in my daily life."

An international gathering of youth met for a full week to discuss how better to promulgate Christ's message to the world. Those assembled for the conference read many informative essays, heard many fine speakers, watched a few videos, and had ample time to discuss with each other. As the conference was beginning to break up and those attending were packing to leave, a young woman from East Africa arose and said, "In my country when we hear that a pagan village is ready to accept the gospel we don't send books, videos, a Bible, or even an evangelist. Rather we send the best Christian family we can find because we have found that the example of a good family speaks louder and more clearly than all the books, speeches, and videos in the world."

These short vignettes all have one common theme: what we do is extremely important. Our actions speak quite plainly to people about who we are and what we profess and believe. Jesus tells his apostles they are salt and light. They are to go forth, make the world a better place by being its salt, and illumine people who live in darkness to the light of Christ's message. The privilege of Christianity carries with it the responsibility of being present to others and assisting them in finding God in our world. We cannot allow ourselves to become salt that has gone flat; we must do nothing that extinguishes the light and leaves people without the illumination of Christ.

Points Of Challenge And Questions To Ponder

1. How do we salt the earth? How do we radiate the light? Jesus' challenge was not merely for his immediate followers; it applies to us in equal measure.

2. What concrete manifestations of service to God's people can we claim? What have we done lately for our brothers and sisters, especially those who suffer the pain of mind, body, or spirit? Service to God's children is of great importance and is the appropriate response to the God who first loved us. We cannot be

true disciples who illumine the face of Christ unless we are willing to serve and be Christ to one another.

3. When people observe us, is the picture they receive the one we wish to portray or something different? Is it clear to those around us that we stand with Jesus? People are not neutral in their opinions of us. Whether we know it or not we are constantly being watched and evaluated by others. What we do and say either draws others closer to God or pushes them farther away. We must be evangelists as the salt and light of Christ.

4. Have we taken our responsibility as Christ's disciples seriously? Do we understand that the privilege of Christianity requires something of us? We cannot escape the reality that any privilege brings responsibility. Christ has given us all things; we are asked to reciprocate and return some of who we are to God and God's people.

5. Do we demonstrate God's love for all people? Do we bring Christ to all our endeavors — family and personal relationships, our schools, our place of work? They say there are no atheists in foxholes, but if we bring Christ to all that we do then there should be no atheists anywhere. Christ is the solution, and thus the Lord must be present in all our efforts. Without Jesus what we do is void of true meaning.

Exegesis And Explanation Of The Parable

This combination of two short metaphorical parables is part of the famous Sermon on the Mount (5:1—7:29), Matthew's first and longest collection of Jesus' teaching, and is a central part of his Gospel. The sermon serves as the frontpiece of Matthew, setting the tone for the entire Gospel. The evangelist presents Jesus as Israel's ultimate teacher, the one who is authorized by God in his ministry. The sermon, beginning with the beatitudes, continuing with a series of teachings, and concluding with a reaction of amazement on the part of those hearing the Lord, warns readers that believing in Jesus means more than listening. Actively following the dictates and teachings of Jesus is necessary. It anticipates the great commission at the conclusion of the Gospel, "Go therefore and make disciples of all nations, baptizing them in the name of the Father and of the Son and of the Holy Spirit, and teaching them to obey everything I have commanded you" (28:19-20a).

Matthew uses the Q (*Quelle*) source to make this sermon Jesus' first great act. Unlike Luke, who places Jesus on a plain when delivering the sermon, Matthew gives the event greater significance by having Jesus deliver his teaching "up the mountain." Matthew uses Jesus' words to make a Christological statement. The sermon tells Christians how they are to live, but it also emphasizes the importance of Jesus himself. He is not simply "one of the prophets"; he is the Messiah. Jesus sits like a king on his throne; his disciples approach him like subjects in a royal court. In this inaugural address to his people, Jesus, the king, describes in considerable detail what life in the kingdom will be like.

Matthew uses the parables of salt and light and the challenge these images present as a transition from the beatitudes to the instructions of 5:17—7:12. The evangelist wants his readers to know that the lessons to come are eschatological; they look forward to the ultimate purpose and final goal of the disciples' vocation. In their Matthean context these images of salt and light serve to illustrate the sacrificial service which the new kingdom will demand of all who follow Jesus.

Salt, a commodity valued as precious as a human life in apostolic times, was, therefore, of great significance to the people of Jesus' day and its image was filled with meaning. Thus, when the Lord calls the apostles the salt of the earth (v.13), he is presenting his chosen followers with a deep and challenging message. As salt gives zest to food, so Christian people have the duty to add joy and hope to the common, everyday occurrences of life. Christians are to bring zest to life through personal relationships, actions, trust, and worship of God. Salt was also used as a principal preservative for foods. As the salt of the earth the apostles are thus called to root out things like greed and lust, which corrupt society, lead to indifference, and ultimately cause decay. Jesus warns his chosen twelve that they must remain centered in him and not become polluted with the words of false teachers. Salt that is impure loses its usefulness: "It is ... thrown out and trampled under foot." As a pinch of salt in food has an influence out of proportion to its size, so the apostles' action to "salt" the earth with teachings of Jesus will produce a great harvest.

In calling the apostles "the light of the world" Jesus reveals the future mission of the apostles as evangelists. For Matthew the image of light refers to the illumination of discipleship. Unlike John, who portrays Jesus as the light, and Luke, who uses the image of light to guide the growth of the Church, Matthew uses light to illumine God. All in the Church are to be disciples who share the light of hope for all tomorrows. The primary task of Christian witness is to be a lighted city on a hill. Matthew has intentionally contrasted the lighting of a lamp with extinguishing it, placing it under a bushel basket. The apostles are called to an active mission: "In the same way, let your light shine before others, so they may see your good works and give glory to your Father in heaven" (v.16). The light is to shine and illumine God, not our own works. This is the essential mission of the Christian.

Matthew's combined use of salt and light images clearly refers to Israel's mission to the nations. The apostle and evangelist believes that Israel to date has failed to carry out the charge given to God's people. Now the Church of Jesus and the Gentiles must take up the task. Understood in their traditional meaning as symbols for the law and God's covenant, the images of salt and light may also serve to demonstrate how Jesus' disciples are to proclaim to the world their Master's new interpretation of the Law and the need for people to live according to this new way.

Context Of The Parable

Context In The Church Year

The parables of salt and light, a continuation of Jesus' Sermon on the Mount begun last week, are used by the church to illustrate the start of Jesus' public ministry as a teacher. In these weeks following the Christmas season the Gospel has described John the Baptist's recognition of Jesus, the call of the first apostles, and the start of the Lord's teaching mission. This is the second of six consecutive Sundays where a semi-continuous reading of the Sermon on the Mount will be undertaken. Moving from the infancy narrative to the start of Jesus' public ministry, this parable and the entire Sermon on the Mount provide the ideal introduction to the Lord's message of peace and love.

Context With Other Gospels
    The parables of salt and light in Matthew are contained in Luke and Mark in different forms. Luke 11:33 speaks of lighting a lamp and placing it on a stand "so that those who enter may see the light" and Luke 14:34-35 describes the image of salt. Mark 9:50 also presents the image of salt. Mark and Luke use truncated versions of these images for their own purposes. Luke does not describe the apostles as salt or light and, therefore, is not interested in using the images to demonstrate the need for service as does Matthew. Similarly, Mark's use of the image of salt is not connected with the ministry of the apostles.

Context With First And Second Lessons
First Lesson: Isaiah 58:1-9a (9b-12). The third section of Isaiah's long book of prophecy, chapters 56-65, was written to the Hebrews after their return from exile in Babylon. The prophet equates assisting others — sharing bread with the hungry, sheltering the oppressed and homeless, and clothing the naked — with the light. When we aid God's people in any way, but especially those who are less fortunate or live on the margins of society, we illumine God's message of love to the world. Service to our fellow men and women brings the light of Christ to a society that often prefers darkness. Isaiah's concrete message provides an illustration as to how Jesus' exhortation in the Gospel to be salt and light can be manifest.

Second Lesson: 1 Corinthians 2:1-12 (13-16). Paul's message to the Corinthians emphasizes the action of God in our world and the need for faith in order to perceive it. He stresses the point that what we do is not ultimately for ourselves, but rather is for God. It is faith, coming from the power of God and not mere human wisdom, that illumines the presence of God in our world. When we as God's people express our faith in word and action, then we bring the light and set it on a stand where it can be seen and thus be useful. Paul is convinced that his understanding of the need for faith is a gift of God's Spirit who acts through him. Paul, like Jesus in the parable, sees human action as a means to illumine the presence of God, but we can only act out of faith. Without faith our actions are personal and not centered in God.

Chapter 2

The Gate Of Life

John 10:1-10

"Very truly, I tell you, anyone who does not enter the sheepfold by the gate but climbs in by another way is a thief and a bandit. The one who enters by the gate is the shepherd of the sheep. The gatekeeper opens the gate for him, and the sheep hear his voice. He calls his own sheep by name and leads them out. When he has brought out all his own, he goes ahead of them, and the sheep follow him because they know his voice. They will not follow a stranger, but they will run from him because they do not know the voice of strangers." Jesus used this figure of speech with them, but they did not understand what he was saying to them.

So again Jesus said to them, "Very truly, I tell you, I am the gate for the sheep. All who came before me are thieves and bandits; but the sheep did not listen to them. I am the gate. Whoever enters by me will be saved, and will come in and go out and find pasture. The thief comes only to steal and kill and destroy. I came that they may have life, and have it abundantly."

Theme

They say that variety is the spice of life and I guess the adage is true. Life would be rather dull if everything were the same and we had no choices. We make decisions of choice each day. Most of our choices are rather mundane — what we will wear, what we will eat, how we will plan our day, what time we will retire to bed.

There are occasions, however, when we must make important decisions that may change or impact our future — what job or occupation we will seek, where we will live, the choice of a spouse, planning a family. The choice of God is placed before us each day. We can say yes or no to God's call; the choice is always ours. The world presents us with many choices, many forks along the road of life, but there is only one option that leads to God and eternal life. We, God's children, must choose Jesus and enter the pasture of life.

Spiritual Food For The Journey

Why does the world suffer? Why do pain, problems, and suffering exist in such abundance? We all believe that God is all good, all love, full of compassion, and all powerful. This is how we define God. We believe this to be true. Thus, the question bears repeating, why does our world suffer? Why do wars exist and people die in innocence? Why do people in positions of public trust commit acts that cause others not only to lose faith in the individual, but in the system as well? Why do people fight one another when the only difference between them is the color of their skin, their political preference, or religious belief?

For me the basic answer to these challenging questions is personal choice, our free will to say yes or no to God at any time in any way. Sören Kierkegaard, the famous nineteenth-century existentialist philosopher and theologian, once wrote, "Faith is a matter of choice, our personal decision in finding God." This personal decision, our free will, is why the world suffers. It is free will that allows the drunk to drive and kill others. It is free will that allows people in public service to break the law and thus lower the integrity of the system. It is free will that places certain members and groups in society on the fringe and does not allow them to participate. Free will moves us closer to or further from God. As Kierkegaard wrote, it is our decision; faith is our choice.

Jesus, the gate that leads to life, invites us follow him to his pasture. Our great gift of free will allows us to say yes or no to God. God loves us so much that we were given the option whether or not we wish to follow the Lord. It some ways it might be easier if we were animals that relied totally on instinct. We would then be programmed to follow the Lord and find eternal life. God, however, believes that the choice must be ours. God wants us to give our daily assent to his invitation. Many will present themselves along the way as the gate we should employ. We must find our way through the maze of false teachers, hopeless situations, and problematic circumstances to find Jesus and the true path which he provides home to God. The choice is ours! Jesus put it well in Matthew's Gospel (7:13-14): "Enter through the narrow gate; for the gate is wide and the road is easy that leads to destruction, and there are many who take it. For the gate is narrow and the road is hard that leads to life, and there are few who find it."

Application Of The Parable To Contemporary Life

Sermon Openings
1. They say that variety is the spice of life, and I suspect that the adage is true. We have a need for variation and change in our lives. Without some differences the world would be a rather boring place. Fortunately variety and differences are commonplace in our world.

The variety that surrounds us requires us to make choices. If we go to the supermarket and take the shopping cart down the aisle where the cereals are stacked high, the choices before us may be rather mind-boggling. Cereals go from the rather mundane to the exotic, from sugar-coated to fiber plus; the choices are seemingly endless. Take a ride down to the local auto mart, located in most large metropolitan areas. We can choose cars from Germany or Japan, Sweden or Korea, England or the United States, just to mention the major dealers. Once we settle on a make, there are almost endless models from which we must choose. We can choose a luxury automobile, an economy-class vehicle, or one in between. We can purchase a sedan, convertible, or a wagon. We can also choose between types of vehicles: cars, trucks, or the very popular sports-utility vehicles.

What criteria do we use to make our choices? The answer certainly depends upon what we are seeking. For most people cost is a major criterion. Practicality is another, but not always. Sometimes we make choices because they are impractical. There are occasions when we want to be outrageous, whether it is the clothes we wear, the car we drive, or the food we eat. With all the choices in almost everything from food to transportation to clothes, we seldom, if ever, need to change or accommodate our desires. If we look hard enough and wide enough, and have the patience to wait, we will obtain exactly what we want.

What is it that separates the human race from the rest of God's creation? Aside from our souls, the best answer is our ability to choose. God gave us free will, but this gift of freedom requires our responsible action. Today's Gospel reading reflects the choice that we must make to discover God and find life through the gate which is Jesus our Lord.

2. Once upon a time a great and loving king ruled over a vast territory. There was something very strange about this kingdom, however. Everything was the same. The people ate the same food, drank the same drink, wore the same clothes, and lived in the same type of homes. The people even did all the same work. There was another oddity about this place. Everything was gray — the food, the drink, the clothes, the houses; there were no other colors.

One day a majestic and very beautiful bird flew from the west into a small village that lay a great distance from the capital city. The bird deposited a yellow egg and flew off. The people were fascinated with their new possession since they had never seen anything but gray. They played with the egg and poked it. In the process the egg broke. Inside was a yellow powder. Anything that came in contact with the powder instantly turned yellow. At the outset a few people's clothes and some other objects turned yellow, but the people were soon so struck with their new discovery that the whole village was "painted" yellow. The next day the same bird flew from the west and deposited a blue egg in another small village. It did not take long before everything in this village was blue. This same scenario repeated itself on seven consecutive days as the majestic bird deposited seven different colored eggs in seven villages.

The great king in the capital city, where all was still gray, heard about these strange events and wondered what the sign might mean. He called in his royal councilors and advisors and asked them if anything like this had happened in the past. They checked the ancient manuscripts and discovered that many generations ago the kingdom was ruled by a philosopher king. At the time there was much dissension, strife, and conflict in the kingdom. It was further discovered that the source of this dissension came about from the differences that existed among the people. The king, who wanted peace, believed that the only way to restore harmony was to eliminate all differences among the people. This is why all the people did the same things and all was gray.

The present king was worried that the various colors in the villages would again lead to dissension and strife. Thus, he ordered the royal archers to locate the majestic bird and slay it. The archers found the bird and their arrows were sent straight and true, but they had no effect on the bird, which simply flew away. If the bird could not be stopped then the people must be, thought the king. Thus, he ordered the people to remove all the colors and return to gray. But the people, who were enamored with the new colors in their lives, refused to obey the king's order. Dissension, strife, and conflict ensued — the very things the king was trying to prevent.

The king was unsure as to what to do until one day the beautiful majestic bird flew into the royal palace and deposited seven different colored eggs. The king was frustrated and angry, and in a fit of rage he hurled the eggs in all different directions. They burst into an array of color. The beauty was so great that the king, in a moment of inspiration, knew precisely what he needed to do. He now realized that the bird was a sign that change was needed, but he had ignored the sign. Thus, the king ordered that all the people must have all the colors. Again there were no differences, and dissension, strife, and conflict ceased. All the people lived happily ever after.[1]

33

John Aurelio's story "Colors" speaks of how a king was given a choice — follow the sign of God or ignore the sign and go your own way. His failure to heed the sign almost brought disaster for him and his kingdom. Jesus in today's Gospel presents us with a choice — will we enter life through him or seek another road? The choice is ours!

Points Of Challenge And Questions To Ponder

1. What are the criteria that we use to make the important decisions of our lives? Do we seek out family and friends, colleagues and associates? What place does God have in our decision making process?

2. What responsibility do we feel for those God has entrusted to us? Young people, students, or subordinates at work all look to elders and superiors to lead them. By following our lead will people find the pasture of life or are we leading people astray by the conduct of our lives?

3. What choices have we made lately? Were they helpful and did they aid us along the path of life or were they destructive? If they were harmful, did we have the courage to change and make a better choice?

4. When we make decisions are they based solely on our needs and wants or do we consider the desires of others? If we find ourselves in positions of authority, do we make choices that are beneficial to all or are we selfish in our choices?

5. Jesus' life demonstrates that suffering is part of the Christian life. Are we willing to make the decision that may cause suffering because it is the right choice, or do we shy away because we are afraid to endure a crisis for the sake of Christ's name?

Exegesis And Explanation Of The Parable

Background To The Gospel Of John

The Gospel of John presents the life, teachings, and message of Jesus in ways unique to the whole of the New Testament. Any serious reader of the Scriptures is familiar with the Synoptic tradition of Matthew, Mark, and Luke, its common sources, consistent chronology of Jesus' life, and literary format, including the frequent use of parables. John's Gospel, written later and for a different audience, presents a distinctive view of Christ, consistent in teaching and understanding with the Synoptics, but with a unique chronology, approach, and style compared with the other three Gospel evangelists.

Authorship of the fourth Gospel has been debated by scholars over the centuries. Ireneaus, Bishop of Lyons (180 AD), was the first to ascribe the account to John the Apostle, a belief that was common in the late second century.[2] Corroboration of apostolic authorship is provided in the text of the Gospel. It is clear that the author is a Jew familiar with Palestine and an eyewitness to the events related. The precision with which the author identifies places, such as the Pool of Bethsaida (5:2), indicates exact knowledge of the region. The nomenclature of the Gospel also reflects the Judean scene before 70 AD, the date of the Roman destruction of the Temple and the Diaspora.

Confusion on authorship comes about when scholars compare the fourth Gospel with other books ascribed to John — his three letters and the Book of Revelation. The Gospel and epistles were physically written by one well-schooled in Greek, while Revelation was penned in a very rough, even crude, form of Greek common to the Semitic tradition of a Galilean fisherman. Additionally, the language and literary tradition of Revelation is much different than the other books ascribed to John the Apostle. In order to explain this disparity, Scripture exegetes have concluded that the Gospel and Epistles of John were actually written by someone employed by the Apostle as a disciple-scribe whose knowledge of Greek was vastly superior to his own. This does not contradict

Johannine authorship, especially when one considers it was quite common in the period for scribes to write in the names of others.

Physical authorship by someone other than John the Apostle is also indicated by textual inconsistencies and additions to the original manuscript. At times in this Gospel the discourses of Jesus are interrupted for no apparent reason. Chapter 14 concludes with Jesus exhorting his disciples to "Rise, let us be on our way," indicating a shift in location and the end of a teaching. Yet, chapter 15 begins with another teaching, "I am the vine," that appears to have been added by a later interpolator. Additions to the original text are seen best in the whole of chapter 21. The Gospel clearly ends with the evangelist's teaching that Jesus did many other things not recorded, yet the book continues with its famous post-Resurrection narrative. Scholars today generally agree that the Gospel of John was dictated over a long period of time, with its completion and final ordering done after the Apostle's death.

Debate over the date and place of composition of John's Gospel has also evolved over time. In the late nineteenth century scholars believed the book to have been composed in the late second century from evidence of influences that were not present in the apostolic age. This belief was bound up with the idea that the Gospel was of little historical value and could not have been the work of an eyewitness. As we have seen above, however, contemporary scholarship has demonstrated the consistency of this Gospel with the Jewish background of the time of John the Baptist and Jesus. The Gospel's use in the writings of Ignatius of Antioch, Justin Martyr, and several references in the Gnostic gospels make it difficult to suggest any date later than the end of the first century for the Gospel's composition. The strongest and most ancient tradition has placed the Gospel's composition at Ephesus.

The Gospel of John, although understood as a separate evangelical effort that relates Jesus' life and message, still maintains important connections to the Synoptic writers. The Synoptic tradition in several ways is assumed by John in his message. He takes it for granted, as one example, that the reader knows the apostles, for the Fourth Gospel provides no introduction. More importantly, John's narrative omits basic data on the life of Christ, including his birth and infancy, and the institution of the Eucharist. The author assumes these items, preferring to concentrate in his prologue on the major theological themes of the book and in chapter 6 on an exposition of Eucharistic theology. Many passages in this Gospel would be unclear without the Synoptic tradition as background. The evangelist's purpose is not to supplement or correct the accounts of Matthew, Mark, and Luke, but rather to give his own testimony without regard to style, chronology, or method of his predecessors.

While a detailed explanation of the characteristics of John's Gospel is beyond our purpose in this overview, it is important to understand how certain ideas of this Gospel are associated with the literary genre of parable. Scholars disagree on whether John uses parables in the same manner as the Synoptics. Exegetes point out that John uses many of the same metaphors and symbols of the other evangelists, but their format is more allegory than parable. Nevertheless, the symbolism, as we will see in the pericope of the gate and the shepherd (John 10:1-10), is quite complex and serves to profess an important message, as do all parables. John's use of symbol is his basic pattern of relating the teachings of Jesus to a wider audience in time and space. The evangelist's use of the symbols of light and dark to represent life and death, Christ against sin, is portrayed throughout the Gospel. Universal symbology is present in characters such as Lazarus and the Beloved Disciple representing all Christians, not merely their historical personages. Mary, the Mother of God, is symbolic for the universal church. The message of the parable in the Synoptics is thus presented through use of symbols in the Gospel of John.

Exegesis Of John 10:1-10

The so-called parable of the sheepgate, John 10:1-5, poses an exegetical problem for biblical scholars in discovering its source and inspiration. While there appear to be connections in symbology between this passage and several verses in the Synoptics, the direct influence is Ezekiel chapter 34, which speaks of how God will send the Messiah to the people (the flock) as its new, true, and good shepherd. Yahweh, in the words of the prophet, condemns the leaders of Israel as negligent shepherds who have grossly abused their office, feeding themselves instead of the people so that the latter have become scattered and are easy prey for thieves and robbers. Yahweh intervenes, the unworthy shepherds are dispossessed, and the Lord takes personal responsibility for the people. God will bring the people home from exile in Babylon.

Drawing from Ezekiel, the evangelist uses new images in this pericope to continue Jesus' assault on the Pharisees initiated in chapter 9. The blind beggar whom Jesus cures (John 9:1-41) is found in chapter 10 in the guise of faithful sheep who recognize and know the shepherd, while the Pharisees are presented as thieves, who only come in order to steal and destroy the sheep, or as hirelings, who abandon the sheep at the first approach of danger. The identification of the Pharisees as the thieves or hirelings of the pericope is questioned by some scholars who suggest the evangelist may be pointing to individuals and groups from the past as well as present claimants to leadership in Israel. Those who falsely claim themselves to be the Messiah may also be envisioned in this polemic.

A description of the daily routine of the shepherd provides the background necessary to understand the symbolism of the parable in verses 1-5. In Jesus' day several flocks of sheep were kept at night in a common corral behind a sturdy gate. A trusted sentry or gatekeeper watched the sheep all night. In the morning the individual shepherds returned to the corral, were recognized by the gatekeeper, and allowed to call the sheep, who only came at the voice of the shepherd. The shepherd in turn led his flock out to pasture during the day. Thus, at night the gate kept the sheep safe while in the day the shepherd was responsible for their welfare.

Verses 1-5 present two separate but important messages. First, there is a polemical warning to all false leaders who may jeopardize the flock of Israel. Secondly, the pericope presents a positive image of the bond between the shepherd and his sheep. This twofold meaning is the guiding principle behind both the arrangement and structure of the passage. Taken as a whole these verses serve the evangelist's intent to raise certain issues that will be explained later (verses 7-18).

Scripture exegetes differ on the sources and method of composition of John 10:1-5. Some believe the pericope to be a combination of two parables with allegorical interpretations presented later in the chapter. Verses 1-3a speak of entering through the gate, while verses 7-10 say Jesus is the gate. The second parable, verses 3b-5, concentrating on the shepherd's role in leading the flock to pasture, is complemented by verses 11-18 where Jesus describes himself as the Good Shepherd. Other scholars suggest that any sharp division in the verses is artificial, as the entire passage focuses on the shepherd and his relation to the flock. A positive image of the shepherd is contrasted against a negative image of the thief and bandits. Here the Pharisees are attacked, not for being false shepherds, but for taking things for themselves at the expense of others. Regardless of the passage's possible origins, its warning appears clear: the authorities must fulfill their role as the watchmen for God's people. This frequent Old Testament theme carries an eschatological urgency expressed in terms of judgment at the gate (Mark 8:29 and Revelation 3:20).

The latter section of John 10:1-10, verses 7-10, like the original parable, has been debated by scholars in recent years. Two basic interpretations of these verses predominate. After Jesus identifies himself as the sheepgate, thus making him the legitimate shepherd of the people, verse 8 suggests the Lord is the gate for the sheep. In verses 9 and 10, however, Jesus is presented as the gate who leads all to salvation and, thereby, the fullness of life. Many scholars see verses 7-10 as an allegory introduced by the disciples' inability to understand (and thus the need for an allegory) in verse 6. Others claim, however, that these verses are not an allegory because of no explicit explanatory correspondence between the two passages.

The message of verses 7-10 was readily apparent to the first hearers of John's Gospel. In Jesus' claim to be the gate, he contrasts his activities with those of thieves and robbers. Jesus facilitates the safe passage of the sheep to proper pastures, but the thieves steal, kill, and destroy the sheep. The true shepherd exists and exercises his authority solely for the good of the sheep, while bandits think of the sheep only in terms of what profit they can make for themselves or how they can best secure their own safety. In verse 10 the evangelist says that the issue of true and false shepherds is one of life and death. The false shepherd is a usurper whose theft of the kingdom will lead to death. Jesus, the true shepherd, however, governs his people rightly, brings them to God, and ensures them more abundant life than any other place or under any other rule. Jesus, the one bringer of salvation, the one way to the Father, is the one true door for the sheep.

Context Of The Parable

Context In The Church Year

The Feast of the Resurrection and the ensuing Easter season are the apex of the liturgical year. Christianity rejoices that the salvific death of the Lord has brought the world the possibility of salvation. In our joy the Sundays of Easter are initially celebrated with Gospels that recall the post-Resurrection accounts. The parable of the sheepgate is used by the church in this festive season to demonstrate our need to take responsibility for our Christian lives and make the right, proper, and personal decision to choose Jesus each and every day as we experience the Christian journey. Jesus' triumph over death is of no use to the one who does not make the conscious choice to enter the pasture through the one and only gate that allows access. In its wisdom the church gives us this Gospel parable to remind us again of our need to make the right choice, the only option that leads to eternal life. The height of our liturgical celebration can only be attained if we say yes to Jesus and follow his lead.

Context With Other Gospels

John's parable of the sheepgate is *sui generis* to his Gospel, but parallels in imagery between this periciope and passages in the Synoptics abound. Verses 1-5 can be compared with Mark 6:34, which describes the crowd following Jesus as "sheep without a shepherd." The parable of the lost sheep, Luke 15:3-7, presents another parallel. The image of a shepherd's care for his followers is presented in Luke 12:32. Matthew 7:13-14 provides the portrait of the narrow gate leading to life against the wide gate that leads to destruction. The concept of allegory is best demonstrated in the Synoptic parable of the sower, Matthew 13:1-9, 18-23 (chapter 4 of this volume), Mark 4:1-9, 13-21, and Luke 8:4-8, 11-15.

Context With First And Second Lessons
First Lesson: Acts 2:42-47. The Acts of the Apostles describes the life of the Christian community after the Resurrection. That event transformed people and their thoughts to greater faith and action. There is no better example in Acts of this transformation than Saint Peter, who denied the Lord three times before his death. Peter fearlessly and boldly proclaimed the power of the Resurrection in his life as he preached to the Jews about Jesus. The Apostle told the people that they must reform their lives and be baptized in the name of Christ. Jesus is the only gate through whom they will find life. Although Jesus was rejected by those to whom he came, there is still opportunity for all to be converted to the reality that Christ is, as he claimed himself, the way, the truth, and the life. We are challenged to enter through the gate that will bring us home to God and to eternal life.

The concept of community practiced by the first Christians was the source of strength for the early church. In many ways it became the gate, the vehicle through which believers found life in God. Thus, as this passage states, the community was of one heart and mind. Members of the community worked together to build God's kingdom on earth.

Second Lesson: 1 Peter 2:19-25. Saint Peter tells us that suffering is part of being a follower of Christ. We are all aware of the martyrs who made the choice in their lives to be true disciples without counting the cost. Anyone who truly seeks to walk in the footsteps of Jesus can expect no better than the Master. Yet, we know that if we have the courage of perseverance we will in the end find a home with the Lord. As Peter says, "By his wounds you have been healed."

In our world today few will ever have to suffer as did the early Christians and the martyrs, but the choices we face are not easy.

The plethora of options makes it easy to drift away from the one choice that we truly need. Peter's suggestion that we once strayed like sheep is true for all of us. The Apostle thus exhorts us to return to Jesus, the true shepherd and guardian of our souls.

---

1. Paraphrased from "Colors," in John Aurelio, *Colors! Stories of the Kingdom* (New York: The Crossroad Publishing Company, 1993), pp. 134-136. Used with permission.

2. Ireneaus also identified the author as "the one whom Jesus loved" (John 13:23). There is no other figure in the Gospel that corresponds to the beloved disciple. This understanding of John as the beloved disciple is commonly held today.

Chapter 3

Anchoring Your Life
In The Lord

Matthew 7:21-29

---

*"Not everyone who says to me, 'Lord, Lord,' will enter
the kingdom of heaven, but only the one who does the will
of my Father in heaven. On that day many will say to me,
'Lord, Lord, did we not prophesy in your name, and cast
out demons in your name, and do many deeds of power in
your name?' Then I will declare to them, 'I never knew
you; go away from me, you evildoers.'*

*"Everyone then who hears these words of mine and
acts on them will be like a wise man who built his house
on rock. The rain fell, the floods came, and the winds
blew and beat on that house, but it did not fall, because it
had been founded on rock. And everyone who hears these
words of mine and does not act on them will be like a
foolish man who built his house on sand. The rain fell,
and the floods came, and the winds blew and beat against
that house, and it fell — and great was its fall!"*

*Now when Jesus had finished saying these things, the
crowds were astounded at his teaching, for he taught them
as one having authority, and not as their scribes.*

Theme

Contrasting images of building or failing to build a house upon
a rock foundation present an important theme of our need for Jesus.
Matthew clearly demonstrates that those who fail to anchor their
lives in the Lord will come to ruin when the storms, winds, and

rains of life come. None of us can escape the many obstacles, detours, potholes, and roadblocks that exist in life. It would be nice, but our voyage through life is not always conducted in fair and calm seas. When the storms arise we must be anchored in the Lord. If we are not securely tied to Jesus' message, we will be swept away in the rush of life and never reach home. We must, therefore, root ourselves in the Lord, who will strengthen us to withstand any and all of life's stormy moments.

Spiritual Food For The Journey

Upon what or whom do you place your hope and trust? When life goes sour and problems seem to surround us, where do we turn? Some people rely upon things when the going gets tough. We live in a very materialistic world; things are visible, tangible, and readily available. There are many things in the world that can aid us when things go wrong, when we feel down, or when the forces of the world seem to surround us with gloom. However, there are things that we often seek as aids which only destroy us. They ravage our attitudes and then attack our actions.

Some people place their hope in others. Certainly when a problem arises it is only natural to seek the guidance of a family member, close friend, neighbor, or work associate. People often help us and give us great advice, especially a person who may have walked the road we now experience. But often we seek solutions to our problems in people and situations that lead us nowhere that is helpful; they direct us 180 degrees away from God.

Some people seek answers to the dilemmas of life in themselves. They shut out everything and everyone. Many of us at times develop the attitude that says, "If I want to get it done, I must do it myself." We cannot place sufficient trust in another that a task will be done or problem solved in the manner or with the speed which we feel is needed.

All of us to a lesser or greater extent need to be converted to the need for God in our lives. As good as things and people can be in finding solutions to the crises of life, we must ultimately place our reliance, trust, and confidence in God. We must anchor ourselves in God, God's message of love, service, and commitment, and the Lord's ever present mercy and forgiveness.

We all know that life will present us with many challenges and storms. Are we prepared to stand tall and endure them or will we be swept away in the tide? The answer must come from each person. Those anchored in the Lord will find a safe harbor; those who are not will be lost forever.

Application Of The Parable To Contemporary Life

Sermon Openings
1. Sophocles, the famous Greek dramatist, graced the world with his many plays. His famous trilogy of *Oedipus Rex, Oedipus at Colonus*, and *Antigone* is his greatest legacy. In this trilogy there is a famous section known as the "Riddle of the Sphinx." In order for Oedipus to gain entry to his desired destination he must solve this famous riddle. The passage is as follows: what has four legs in the morning, two legs in the afternoon, and three legs in the evening? The answer is a human being. In the morning, the first period of our life, we crawl; we need all fours, our arms and legs, to move and get around. In the great middle or afternoon of our life we walk upright on two legs. In the twilight of our life we again need some assistance, such as a cane or a helping hand; we use three legs in this stage of our life.

The "Riddle of the Sphinx" tells us something powerful about our reliance on others. When we are infants we need the support of others. We are totally dependent as young children on others, for food, clothing, shelter, love — all our needs. As children we trust that all will be provided. We don't worry; our trust is absolute in those who care for us. When we are old enough to walk, then we begin to rely on ourselves. We venture out, just a little at first, but later with ever more bold steps. We try things for ourselves. As time goes on our ability to trust in others begins to wane. Life throws us curves; we get knocked down and kicked around. Our trust shifts to a more exclusive reliance on the tangible and visible things of our world. We begin to say that we need to do it ourselves; we cannot rely on others any longer. Others just might not come through for us! When we get older, when we need that third leg, we again begin to trust in others. We can no longer do everything that we once could do. We need the aid of other people, for the complex and sometimes even the simple everyday tasks of life.

All of us to some extent need to be converted to a greater reliance on the Lord. The anchor that we need, the base for our life, must be found in the Lord. The parable of the two builders related by Saint Matthew contrasts those who build on the rock of Jesus and those who fail in this task.

2. He was chained, held bound in a life of torment and blasphemy. In the end, however, God would set him free. John Newton, a name probably not familiar to many of us, was born in July, 1725, to a pious English woman and her seafaring husband. From his earliest days, young Newton was attracted to his father's side of the family and to the life at sea. Thus, when he was only eleven years old he became an apprentice aboard his father's vessel, a cargo ship which ferried products throughout the major ports of the Mediterranean region. To say the least, at this time in his life John Newton did not know God. Those with whom he associated for the most part on his father's ship were criminals, rogues, and other "undesirables" of society, many of whom were sent to Captain Newton's ship as punishment for some offense in the State of England.

When Newton was nineteen he became a midshipman on another vessel. After only one year, however, he was publicly flogged for insubordination. Despite this event, and most probably with the help of his father, John was able to secure a commission and a few years later his own vessel, a slave trading ship. John Newton commanded a vessel which ferried Africans from their native land to the American colonies. He was good at what he did. He carried out his duties fully and with precision. Still, he felt chained, trapped; he was unable to release himself.

This all changed one night in 1748. That evening while at sea Newton's slave ship was caught in a vicious storm. Waves crashed over the bow and the ship was tossed about like a toy. Through the skill of the captain and his crew, the ship and all personnel were saved. The experience, however, changed Newton forever. He felt the chains that held him bound begin to weaken. It took seven more years, but finally in 1755 John Newton gave up the slave trade and his life at sea. That same year he met John Wesley and George Whitefield, two Anglican clergymen, who at that time were the leaders in the evangelical revival which would lead to the foundation of Methodism in the United States. In 1764 Newton himself was ordained an Anglican priest. He became a well-known preacher and was one of the first members of what later became known as the Abolitionist movement, with such leaders as Daniel O'Connell in Ireland and William Lloyd Garrison in the United States. It was in 1779, however, that Newton wrote some famous words, autobiographical in nature, that are familiar to us all. "Amazing grace, how sweet the sound that saved a wretch like me. I once was lost, but now I'm found, was blind, but now I see." Yes, John Newton wrote the lyrics that became "Amazing Grace." He was held bound in a life he did not want. In the end, God was the one who set him free.

The life of John Newton serves as a good example to illustrate the message of today's Gospel that we must find our roots in Jesus and his message of peace, love, and service to one another.

Points Of Challenge And Questions To Ponder

1. When you feel adrift in your life, where do you turn? Some people turn to things, some to others, and some rely totally on themselves. We who bear the name Christian, however, are challenged to place our hope in the Lord.

2. Captains of ships at sea that need assistance in guiding a vessel through a storm may command, "Let go the anchor!" If the anchor when released hits a sandy bottom the ship continues to drift. The anchor must find rock in order to steady the vessel. Do we rely on solutions which are sand and only slow our drift, or do we seek the rock, Jesus, who can stabilize us immediately?

3. Do we solve the problems that we encounter with Band-Aids® that eventually come loose and need a second application or do we seek more permanent solutions which can be found in faith in Jesus? God calls us to seek a more permanent solution to the obstacles and roadblocks we encounter. Jesus is depending on us, his disciples today, to carry on his work in building the Kingdom of God on earth.

4. Do our actions demonstrate that we are Christians? Do we back up our verbal convictions with service to our brothers and sisters? The Lord asks us to respond to his commandment to love as he has loved us.

5. Are our actions motivated by our faith or do we perform so others will notice us? In today's world seeking attention and acclaim for what we do is almost natural. We must avoid the popular urge to feel important and strive instead to be servants, imitating Jesus, who "came not to be served but to serve, and to give his life a ransom for many" (Matthew 20:28b).

Exegesis And Explanation Of The Parable

This parable serves as the climax of Matthew's eschatological discourse and the end of the Sermon on the Mount. The evangelist uses this pericope to set the tone for the rest of his Gospel — namely that it is necessary for a true disciple of the Lord to manifest one's devotion to Christ by obeying his instructions in demonstrations of Christian love and service. Matthew thus suggests that true followers of the Lord must act and not merely listen. Disciples of Christ must respond in love to God and God's people in imitation of Jesus, the one who first loved us.

The opening section of this pericope, verses 21-23, presents an obvious teaching for all who choose to follow the Lord. It is clear that Jesus tells his disciples that he will exclude from the Kingdom of God all who fail to do the will of the Father. In the day of Jesus' return some may call him by name and point to their religious deeds, but because of their failure to do the Father's will they will have no part in the Kingdom. No act, however great in appearance, can guarantee salvation if it is not based on the foundation of Jesus' teaching that expresses the Father's will.

Besides the seemingly obvious instruction, these opening verses also pose two interesting theological questions. Scholars have proposed different interpretations as to Christ's role at the time of the eschaton. Is Jesus the eschatological judge or an advocate who testifies for or against his followers at the time of the last judgment? Most exegetes argue that the latter interpretation is the intent of the passage. Judgment will be based on one's obedience to the will of the Father. Another question posed by these two verses concerns the Messiahship of Jesus. Some scholars argue that this is Matthew's first attempt to reveal the messianic purpose of Jesus' ministry by demonstrating his relationship with the Father. However, most believe that Peter's confession of faith (Matthew 16:18) is the climactic element in this Gospel and serves to define Jesus' Messiahship.

The heart of this passage, verses 24-27, sharply contrasts two ways to respond to Jesus' teaching. The outstanding church leader — those who cry out Lord, Lord — have indeed heard Jesus' words time and again, but they have refused to make Christ's teaching the rule for their lives. As a result their reputation as leaders is built on nothing more than shifting sand. On the other hand, those humble disciples who can claim no special gifts, rank, or education, but who listen intently to Jesus' words and strive to live by them, have built their lives upon the rock that withstands the storms of life and of the final judgment. The important point for Matthew is that activity which originates from and is an interpretation of Jesus' words represents a decision that the Lord's teaching is the ground on which to build. One hearer of Christ's message uses it as the base of life for all our actions; the other hearer has decided that Jesus is not the base upon which to build. As the torrential autumn rains accompanied by the storm test the foundations of the house, so the vicissitudes and obstacles of our daily existence will put one's life to the test. The one who uses Jesus as the base will endure; the other person will be destroyed. In short, Jesus' teaching is the only secure basis for life.

This center section of the passage makes some extraordinary claims for the teaching of Jesus. It is implied that he speaks with more than human authority. A life built upon observance of Jesus' message is secure against all assaults; the life that fails to carry out Jesus' words is fated to utter ruin. Thus, Matthew is suggesting that the Lord's words possess great power and authority. One must not only know the law, one must place the law into action.

This pericope ends with a profound statement on the importance of Jesus' message and its impact on people who hear it. The daring nature and finality of Jesus' teaching becomes clear when Matthew reports that the people were astonished at what they heard. Jesus must have presented a great contrast to the teaching of the rabbis. The rabbis' counsel concerned the knowledge of the Law and following the Commandments. Matthew thus demonstrates in this section that mere knowledge of the Torah was unprofitable and a life devoted to it insecure unless action accompanied it. Some scholars see this section as Matthew's way of making a Christological statement. The reaction of the people tells the reader that what has just been presented by Jesus in the Sermon on the Mount is not merely the understanding of a wise teacher, but the instructions of the Messiah. Combined with verses 21-23, this ending forms a framing of an important teaching of Jesus on the need to anchor one's life in the Lord by two separate statements that speak of Jesus' messianic role.

Situated at the end of the Sermon on the Mount, Matthew wants his readers to understand fully that Jesus demands doers, not just hearers, of the word. Merely listening to the Lord's words is insufficient. The believer must take Jesus at his word and build a house of faith on Jesus alone. Whoever is wise listens seriously and finds direction in life in Jesus' message. Whoever listens to Jesus but does not take his words into practice comes to utter ruin. Such a person has not taken time to lay the proper foundation, a failure which will lead to destruction.

Context Of The Parable

Context In The Church Year

The parable of the two builders, the conclusion of the Sermon on the Mount, is presented in the post-Easter season. Jesus' emphasis on the need to build one's life on him and his teaching serves as a springboard for us to go forth and carry out this challenging mission. Pentecost or Ordinary Time is a period when the basic teachings of the Lord are presented to build upon the foundation of faith which was constructed at our baptism. Thus, this parable serves to remind us of the need always to keep our lives and what we do centered on Jesus' message. The challenge we receive this week keeps us on our toes, ready to meet the vicissitudes and storms of life which threaten to derail us and keep us from our goal.

Context With Other Gospels

The parable of the two builders is contained in the Gospel of Luke (6:47-49) as well as Matthew. Although the two versions appear at first reading to be the same on most counts, there are important differences that demonstrate the different audiences addressed and the message that each evangelist wanted to present. Luke wrote for Hellenists in Asia Minor and other parts of the Mediterranean world. Writing for his audience, unfamiliar with the terrain of Palestine and thus the images used by Matthew, may be the reason that he emphasizes construction, "because it had been well built," (verse 48) over site. Luke mentions no rain or wind, only a rising river, in his account. These were most probably the climatic conditions that Luke's audience experienced. Matthew, on the other hand, preserves the Palestinian setting of the Q source and is more Hebraic in his rendition. The two house sites, not good and poor construction practices, are important to Matthew. The choice of Jesus as the rock foundation is the emphasis of Matthew; Luke is more concerned with what the builder (you and me) does. Both evangelists thus are concerned with a human response to Jesus' message, but Matthew is more concerned with the base and Luke the work.

Context With First And Second Lessons

First Lesson: Deuteronomy 11:18-21, 26-28. In the first reading the church has chosen a passage from the Pentateuch or Torah that expresses the same contrast presented by Matthew on obedience to God. Moses tells the people that those who obey the commandments of the Lord will be blessed and those who refuse obedience will be rewarded with a curse. The people are given a choice; neither God nor Moses will command loyalty. As with Jesus' words in Matthew's Gospel, this passage from Deuteronomy implies that obedience will bring one to God. If the Lord blesses one for obedience and curses one who refuses to obey, the choice is obvious.

Second Lesson: Romans 1:16-17, 3:22b-28 (29-31). Matthew's exhortation to build one's life on the rock foundation of Jesus is supported and enhanced by this section of Paul's Letter to the Romans. The apostle to the Gentiles tells us that God's justice comes to those who possess faith in Jesus — those who build their houses on his solid foundation. It is through Jesus that we have found justification, not by what we have done, but through Christ's salvific death. Paul thus balances the need for works with God's more basic call to faith. Works performed in response to the God who loved us and died for us can only be efficacious when they are performed in faith. Faith and works can serve as a pattern for the Christian life in its daily practice.

Chapter 4

Persistence Along
The Road Of Life

Matthew 13:1-9, 18-23

That same day Jesus went out of the house and sat beside the sea. Such great crowds gathered around him that he got into a boat and sat there, while the whole crowd stood on the beach. And he told them many things in parables, saying: "Listen! A sower went out to sow. And as he sowed, some seeds fell on the path, and the birds came and ate them up. Other seeds fell on rocky ground, where they did not have much soil, and they sprang up quickly, since they had no depth of soil. But when the sun rose, they were scorched; and since they had no root, they withered away. Other seeds fell among thorns, and the thorns grew up and choked them. Other seeds fell on good soil and brought forth grain, some a hundredfold, some sixty, some thirty. Let anyone with ears listen!

"Hear then the parable of the sower. When anyone hears the word of the kingdom and does not understand it, the evil one comes and snatches away what is sown in the heart; that is what was sown on the path. As for what was sown on rocky ground, this is the one who hears the word and immediately receives it with joy; yet such a person has no root, but endures only for a while, and when trouble or persecution arises on account of the word, that person immediately falls away. As for what was sown among thorns, this is the one who hears the word, but the cares of the world and the lure of wealth choke the word, and it yields nothing. But as for what was sown on good

*soil, this is the one who hears the word and understands
it, who indeed bears fruit and yields, in one case a hundredfold, in another sixty, and in another thirty."*

Theme

The parable of the sower and its interpretation present us with
two diverse themes. The parable itself, verses 1-9, is an exhortation to persistence against opposition. Despite the difficulties in
life that produce unfruitfulness in certain venues, those who courageously accept the challenge to continue to sow, to maintain one's
goals and work, will produce an abundant harvest, a yield which
only God can provide.

The allegorical interpretation of the parable, verses 18-23, suggests the need to stand strong against temptation, tribulation, and
defeat in order to produce a rich harvest. Understanding God's
word and appropriating it as a part of one's life will reap a wonderful reward. Strength in the face of opposition will bring one home
to God.

Spiritual Food For The Journey

All of us as children learned the famous tale of "The Little
Engine That Could" and its simple but profound message of the
need to persevere. We are also familiar with the Gospel story of
the persistent woman who kept pestering the judge until he ruled
in her favor (Luke 18:1-8). Perseverance, persistence, and constant
vigilance to the task are virtues of great importance in today's world,
which often frustrates, almost on a daily basis, our will to negotiate
the many obstacles and detours we face. If we do not demonstrate
a persistent attitude in the way we approach life, then we will surely
be defeated. One cannot expect to succeed in a task, whether it be
running a mile under six minutes, publishing an article, convincing
a relative or friend that he must seek professional guidance, or
feeling confident about God's call in one's life, on the first effort.
Those who possess the ability to come back again and again to the
task at hand will be the ones who will experience victory in the

end. The persistence of God's search for us, leaving no stone unturned in an effort to find us and bring us home, must be the model we use in our daily walk with the Lord. We must doggedly pursue all our endeavors as aggressively as Francis Thompson's immortal "Hound of Heaven" pursues our soul, never tiring and without rest.

As well as being persistent in our efforts, we must never be defeated by opposition. The world can be a cruel place which seems anything but hospitable, especially to those who desire to walk with the Lord. We will get knocked down, proverbially to our knees, on numerous occasions in life, but the true Christian is one who refuses simply to lie in the dust, but rather picks oneself up, dusts off, and continues to move along the road that leads to life. We may at times think that we walk alone, that God has forgotten us, but God is ever faithful. As the Scriptures relate: "If we have died with him, we will also live with him; if we endure, we will also reign with him; if we deny him, he will also deny us; if we are faithless, he remains faithful — for he cannot deny himself" (2 Timothy 2:11-13). The anonymous author of the poem "Footprints" understood our relationship with God: "The Lord replied, 'My son, my precious child, I love you and I would never leave you. During your times of trial and suffering, when you see only one set of footprints, it was then that I carried you.' "

Application Of The Parable To Contemporary Life

Sermon Openings
1. For the theme of persistence:

History records the expression, *Athanasius contra mundum* — Athanasius against the world. These words aptly express the situation in the fourth century Church when heresy almost reigned supreme — save Athanasius, a bishop who was a persistent and staunch defender of the faith. Athanasius was born into a Christian family in Alexandria, Egypt, in 295 AD. In his early twenties he was ordained and entered the service of Alexander, bishop of Alexandria. He accompanied the bishop to the first ecumenical council of the church at Nicaea when, among other matters, the heresy of Arianism, which promoted the idea that Jesus was not God, was first condemned.

Three years later in 328, Alexander died and Athanasius was selected as the new bishop of Alexandria. It was at this time that his life as a persistent defender of the faith began. His first opponent was Melitius, a fellow bishop, who believed that it was wrong for the Church to welcome back those who had apostacized. His greatest nemesis, however, was the Arians, who although condemned continued to grow and attract many to their theological perspective. In fact, the number of Arians was so great that Saint Jerome, the original translator of the Scriptures into the Latin (the Vulgate), once wrote, "The world awoke and found itself Arian."

Between 335 and 366 Athanasius, as one of the few bishops in the eastern church who held the orthodox faith, was exiled on five different occasions for a total of seventeen years. Trumped-up charges, false testimony, and the events of the day combined to work against Athanasius. But each time that he returned from exile he was that much more determined to defend the true faith. During his exiles he wrote many important treatises, including *The Life of Antony*, a biography of Antony of the Desert, one of the first desert monks and a precursor to the monastic life. Through tenacity, perseverance, and the fact that he was able to outlive almost all his opponents, Athanasius, in the end, was able to prevail. He died in 373, living his last seven years in relative peace. His greatest triumph came, however, in 381 at the Council of Constantinople when the Nicene-Constantinopolitan Creed, the one professed each Sunday in our churches, was written and accepted. It was a testimony to Athanasius' persistence and dedication. He triumphed, became a saint, and inherited eternal life.

Saint Athanasius' life provides a good example of what today's Gospel describes, that persistence, which is neceesary in all that we do, will be rewarded — thirty, sixty, a hundredfold.

2. For the theme of understanding God's word, appropriating it to one's life, despite opposition:

Three sisters lived in the forest. The oldest was named Bean Plant, the middle sister was named Marigold, and the youngest's name was Lily. It was summer; the weather was beautiful and all who lived in the forest were happy and gay.

Bean Plant, the eldest sister, was one who attracted a lot of attention in the forest. She provided something that attracted all the animals to her. She provided them with food, the lush and rich beans which she produced so abundantly. All the squirrels, rabbits, and other animals came and ate their meals at Bean Plant's house. Bean Plant was proud; she found importance in what she had produced.

Marigold, the middle sister, was also very popular. She produced nothing of value, but she attracted a lot of attention nonetheless. The reason was that Marigold was radiantly beautiful. The gold, yellow, and orange blossoms which she produced brought her many suitors. They were all tall, dark, and handsome and had names of spruce, elm, and oak. Marigold lived in her radiant beauty as the summer days passed.

The youngest sister, Lily, did not attract a lot of attention. She produced no fruit; she was not radiantly beautiful. Lily was short, skinny, and just plain green. Lily had one other habit which her sisters thought was odd; she was constantly talking with the sun. Each day the two friends spoke on several occasions. At dawn when the sun rose in the eastern sky Lily said, "Good morning," and the sun answered, "Good morning, I hope you slept well." Lily spoke with the sun at midday when it was high overhead and bathed the forest with its warm rays. She also spoke to her friend when the sun was on the western horizon, saying, "Good night, thanks for the day. See you tomorrow." Bean Plant and Marigold thought their sister was odd. "You can't speak with the sun," they insisted. But Lily always resisted the opposition of her sisters, replying, "Maybe yes, maybe no, but I will continue to talk with my friend the sun."

One day Lily came to her two older sisters; she was in tears. "The sun is dying," she said, "the sun is dying." Now her sisters truly knew that Lily was crazy. How can the sun be dying? It comes up every day and goes down each night. The sun is strong and powerful, how can it be dying? But, what of it, the older sisters said. We really don't need the sun after all. Yet, Lily insisted that it was true, the sun had told her. Bean Plant and Marigold had to agree about two things, however. The sun seemed to come up a little later and go down a little earlier each day. Additionally, they noticed that the sun was not as high in the sky as it had been earlier. It just was not as warm these days in the forest. "But what of it?" they said. "We don't really need the sun."

As the warmth of the summer months turned into the cooler months of autumn Lily continued to speak with her friend the sun. One fall day there came a strong driving wind which rushed through the forest. The wind blew the beauty that once was Marigold all over the forest. Her suitors no longer thought her attractive. They lost their interest in her, dropped their leaves, and decided to sleep for the rest of the winter. A couple weeks later the first frost came to the forest. The fruit which Bean Plant produced began to shrivel up; it was no longer attractive to the animals of the forest. They too decided to sleep for the winter. One day the cold became so intense that Bean Plant was snapped off at the base; she was no more. But before the sun's strength went away totally, it bent down and kissed its friend Lily and said, "Thank you for talking with me. I love you very much." With that winter came to the forest with all its fury.

After a few months life once again began to appear in the forest. The snows melted and streams again began to run freely. Budding leaves appeared on the trees and the animals again began to forage for food. And there in the middle of the forest appeared one day the most beautiful snow white Lily. As the sun arose in the eastern sky Lily turned and opened her beautiful flower to her friend and said, "Thank you for talking with me. I love you too."[1]

The story of Lily and her two sisters shows the contrast between one who places trust in God and others who cannot. In a world which opposes the Christian message and often frustrates our efforts, we must learn the need to overcome the obstacles of life, always to speak with the Son, so as to find our way home to God.

Points Of Challenge And Questions To Ponder

1. How persistent are we in working toward the achievement of our goals? Do we expect instant results with our projects or are we willing to try again and again as might be necessary?

2. How persistent are we in speaking with God? Often we become frustrated in prayer because that which we seek does not arrive or happen in the way we wish or in the time frame we expect. God is ever vigilant, but we must always remember that God does not operate on the human clock or answer as we often "demand."

3. How patient are we in the conduct of our daily lives? Impatience is often rooted in a lack of perseverance. We want things now; we are unwilling to wait. The parable of the sower suggests that we must continue our efforts without losing heart or patience.

4. What are our expectations in life? All of us have expectations — of situations, events, and especially people. High expectations are good because they challenge us to look to the best and not the worst. However, high expectations are a two-edged sword; the good comes with the bad, namely the possibility that an expectation may not be met. Unfulfilled expectations bring disappointment. It is not the situation, event, or person that is problematic, but rather the level of our expectation that causes us difficulty.

5. When the challenges of life in their varied forms become obstacles and create roadblocks in our lives, what is the solution we seek? Do we seek human solutions or do we place our hope and trust in God? Is God's word with its message of hope our refuge and strength in time of need?

Exegesis And Explanation Of The Parable

Scholars who study the parables of Jesus, despite their many and varied interpretations of Christian history, have made two general conclusions. First, many of the parables, as they are related in the accounts of the four evangelists, are reinterpretations by writers living in the post-resurrection experience of the church. Second, the parables were not intended to be allegorical, but rather, they were intended to make one point only. Biblical commentators today maintain, therefore, that to discover Jesus' original intention it is necessary to remove allegorical interpretations that have been created in attempts to apply the message of the parable to a contemporary context.

The parable of the sower, Matthew 13:1-9, and its allegorical interpretation, 13:28-23, present an excellent example of the problem of understanding Jesus' original intent against an interpretation written at a later time to apply to a different situation. The actual parable, verses 1-9, accurately describes Jesus' own experience. He preached the word, his message of a new covenant, with great persistence and unfailing devotion. Jesus echoed a long tradition in the Hebrew Scriptures of God as sower (Genesis 1:11-12, Jeremiah 31:27, and Hosea 2:23) in this parable. God was ever faithful to the Hebrews. The Lord sent prophets to proclaim God's message, was patient, gave people their freedom to act, and forgave the people's transgressions as the Jews transformed their lives along the direction given by God. Despite some losses, God has produced a rich harvest in the people through persistence. As an observation in history, the parable could be understood that in the history of Israel, in spite of barren periods and unfruitful areas of life, God had never ceased to raise up prophets and leaders to continue the sowing, leading to a rich harvest.

Those who heard this parable could observe in their own lives that in spite of the inevitable loss of some seed, the rewards are so abundantly great that the sower finds it worthwhile to sow year after year, knowing that the harvest will outweigh the loss. The failure of some of the seed to reach maturity and bear fruit was simply an illustration of the frustrations that a farmer must face. The parable, without its explanation, ends on a positive note, a super-abundant harvest. Farmers in the apostolic era considered a yield of ten to one to be good. Thus, Jesus' suggestion of thirty, sixty, or a hundredfold demonstrates how fruitful one's efforts will be if such an endeavor is sustained. As God has been ever faithful and persistent in seeking out the Hebrews, so the Jews of Jesus' age could see the need to be persistent in their daily tasks as well. Additionally, the parable spoke to the people of how God remained faithful through the person, message, and ministry of Jesus. Spiritual unfruitfulness will always be manifest, yet God's word will have an abundant result. Jesus will be persistent in his message despite opposition by some and a lack of fruit in others. The parable of the sower was preached by Jesus to strenghten his followers against discouragement in the face of opposition.

The allegorical interpretation of the parable of the sower, verses 18-23, presents a picture that is inconsistent with the pericope's original meaning. These verses associate the difficulties of natural hazards experienced by a sower with the causes in daily life for the frequent failure of the Christian evangelist to win converts who will remain steadfast. These verses make no reference to the abundance of the harvest which more than rewards the sower for all efforts. The allegorist is more interested in illustrating the various ways in which people who hear the gospel fail to endure and bear fruit as Christians. The interpretation thus moves away from the positive message of abundance created through persistence to a concentration on the forms of failure.

Most commentators see the allegory as a secondary development of oral tradition. The parable is simple, direct, and natural while the interpretation is a standard allegory. In the parable everything mentioned belongs to the local scene, while in the interpretation outside interests come in at every point. Allegorical language is present throughout verses 18-23 — "receive it with joy," "endures only for a while," "care of the world," "lure of wealth." The author of this allegory may have placed more emphasis on the need to avoid failure when it became clear that Jesus and the early church had failed to win the majority to the new message. The allegory's interpretation is clear to most commentators: Those who receive the word and understand it, that is, have appropriated it intellectually and through commitment in the depths of the heart, will be able to withstand the onslaught of temptation and tribulation and, in the end, produce a bountiful harvest in terms of good fruits of obedience to God's will.

Many Scripture scholars see the parable of the sower as the parable of parables. It is not necessarily the most outstanding of this Gospel literary genre, but it is four parables in one. Yet, all four parts (seed on path, rocks, thorns, and good soil) are all aspects of one significant truth: the word of God is proclaimed and causes a division among those who hear. Some of God's people receive the word, understand it, and obediently fulfill it; others fail to listen because of a hardened past, a basic superficiality, or a vested interest in riches and possessions. These people fail to bear fruit, and even what they have — spiritually speaking — will be taken away from them. The parable, therefore, touches people who are truly in the church and those who are "outside." In the end, however, the faithful proclamation of the gospel will never fail to bring forth an abuandant harvest of fruit — thirty, sixty, or a hundredfold.

Context Of The Parable

Context In The Church Year

With the celebration of the Paschal Mystery long past and the preparation time of Advent far in the future, the church finds itself in a period of no special celebration. While there is never anything ordinary about our community worship, this period of Pentecost or Ordinary Time can at times become routine. Like anything in life that is not marked by special events, people, or circumstances, this period in the church liturgical year requires a bit more effort on our part to celebrate worthily.

The parable of the sower, with its original theme of persistence, is an important message on any occasion, but especially at a time when we may become complacent. Jesus' message of the need to continue along the road, despite life's difficulties and times of barrenness, encourages us to persevere in our daily walk with the Lord. Despite the obstacles, the person who makes the effort to continue on course will produce an abundance today and one day to eternal life.

Context With Other Gospels

The parable of the sower, found in all the synoptics (Mark 4:1-9, 13-20 and Luke 8:4-8, 11-15) is certainly one of the best known, yet least understood. The misunderstanding is explained by the fact that over the centuries the allegorical interpretation offered by each evangelist has been more popular and apparently of greater use than the parable itself. The fact that the synoptic writers all presented this parable demonstrates the importance of its message to their varied audiences.

Each version of the basic parable and its interpretation provides certain elements of importance to its original hearers. Scholars believe the Markan version to be the original. In this version Jesus provides the fullest account of the parable's interpretation. Like Matthew, Mark stresses the pedagogical aspect of the parable and its application in contemporaneous times. Luke's version is abbreviated but contains all the essential elements of the Markan and Matthean parables. Each evangelist in his interpretation uses different language to speak of the seed: Matthew calls it the "word of the kingdom," Mark uses "the word," and Luke refers to the seed as "the word of God." Matthew thus uses eschatological language, Mark maintains his emphasis on the person of Jesus as teacher, and Luke stresses the importance of the Lord's message.

Context With First And Second Lessons

First Lesson: Isaiah 55:10-13. The poetic words of Isaiah the prophet speak clearly to us of the efficacious nature of the word of God. As the rains water the seed that is sown, allowing it to bear much fruit, so God's word, the message proclaimed by Isaiah and all the prophets, will achieve its rightful purpose. God, through the words of Isaiah, wants the Hebrews to know that they must nurture their lives on God's word. The message of God will provide the sustenance needed to overcome all obstacles. For the Hebrews, living in exile in Babylon, this message brought hope that God had not abandoned them. If the people keep faith, God, who has ever been faithful, will sustain them and bring the people home. God's message will save the people.

Second Lesson: Romans 8:1-11. Saint Paul's message to the Christian community at Rome is filled with hope. The people to whom Paul wrote, as the apostle himself, lived under the shadow of constant scrutiny by officials of a pagan government that was not open to the new Christian way. Paul knew the people were suffering, but it was not without hope, for one day the people will share in the glorious freedom which will only come to God's children. Paul exhorts the Romans to place their confidence in the spirit, not in the flesh. To do this it is necessary to realize that God is ever present but that we must persevere in order to discover the Lord. We may find ourselves in different places along the path of life at various points, but we must always be vigilant in our quest for God. God will never give up on us; we can never give up on God or ourselves.

───────────

1. Paraphrase from "Lily" in Walter Wangerin, Jr., *Ragman and Other Cries of Faith* (San Francisco: Harper & Row, Publishers, 1984), pp. 44-52.

Chapter 5

Seeking Greater Tolerance And Patience

Matthew 13:24-30, 36-43

He put before them another parable: "The kingdom of heaven may be compared to someone who sowed good seed in his field; but while everybody was asleep, an enemy came and sowed weeds among the wheat, and then went away. So when the plants came up and bore grain, then the weeds appeared as well. And the slaves of the householder came and said to him, 'Master, did you not sow good seed in your field? Where, then, did these weeds come from?' He answered: 'An enemy has done this.' The slaves said to him, 'Then do you want us to go and gather them?' But he replied, 'No; for in gathering the weeds you would uproot the wheat along with them. Let both of them grow together until the harvest; and at the harvest time I will tell reapers, collect the weeds first and bind them in bundles to be burned, but gather the wheat into my barn.' "

Then he left the crowds and went into the house. And his disciples approached him, saying, "Explain to us the parable of the weeds of the field." He answered, "The man who sows the good seed is the Son of Man; the field is the world, and the good seed are the children of the kingdom; the weeds are the children of the evil one, and the enemy who sowed them is the devil; the harvest is the end of the age, and the reapers are angels. Just as the weeds are collected and burned up with fire, so will it be at the end of the age. The Son of Man will send his angels,

65

*and they will collect out of his kingdom all causes of sin
and all evildoers, and they will throw them into the furnace
of the fire, where there will be weeping and gnashing of
teeth. Then the righteous will shine like the sun in the
kingdom of their Father. Let anyone with ears listen!"*

Theme

We live in an intolerant and impatient world. We almost demand things and we "request" them on our own terms. Many people
will not stand for anything less. A minimum period of reflection,
however, tells us that God's ways are not our ways, and God's
time is not our time. In the parable of the wheat and tares we are
challenged to allow God to act in the world, to be more tolerant of
others and patient as we wait, always trusting in the end that God
will triumph over evil.

Spiritual Food For The Journey

First-world nations like the United States are blessed with such
an abundance of everything that there is a great tendency toward
specific expectations. Expectations of situations, people, and events
lead to disappointment or even anger when things do not turn out
as we plan. Unfulfilled expectations demonstrate the impatience
and intolerance which many people display, simply because we
have grown accustomed to certain things. This is found in the
routine and mundane as well as the more critical aspects of life.
When the mail or daily paper "always" arrives at a specific time
and for some reason the time lapses on a particular day, we become impatient. "The mailman is supposed to be here," we declare to ourselves. If we are accustomed to viewing a certain pro-
gram each week on television and on one occasion there is a change,
we become intolerant, frustrated, or angry. More importantly, we
become intolerant with people (individuals or groups) simply because they are different, disagree with our ideas, or somehow don't
fit our model of what is right and proper.

Impatience and intolerance are the root causes of many social sins, including racism, poverty, and nativism. As a nation of immigrants one might think that Americans collectively would be more tolerant of diversity than other peoples, but sadly this is not the case. Racism and nativism that target immigrants and ethnic and religious minorities have long and infamous histories in our nation. Slavery, anti-Semitism, racial segregation, and anti-Catholicism illustrate how America as a nation has at times failed its own citizens. While the nation has made great strides in the past few generations to eliminate many of these evils, their root causes will always present a challenge. We need to be mindful of where we have been in order to proceed forward in a manner that will help us walk as true disciples of the Lord.

The parable of the wheat and tares presents our contemporary world with a great challenge to root out impatience and intolerance from our individual lives and that of the Christian community as a whole. Jesus tells us that we must be patient with the weeds; there is a chance that they may change and be converted. We cannot live as an exlusive community, but one that welcomes all in a true spirit of Christian love. When we look at our world and its many problems — violence and war, sickness and ignorance, corruption and crime, insensitivity and non-cooperation — we may become discouraged and say, "Why should we try?" The parable tells us, however, that in the end God will triumph and evil will be vanquished. Our task, therefore, is to stay on the road, persevere, and never lose hope. We are called to a change of heart in being more patient and tolerant with ourselves, others, and ultimately God.

Application Of The Parable To Contemporary Life

Sermon Openings

1. Joseph Girzone, the popular priest-author, tells the following story in his parable *Joshua and the Children.*[1] Over a hundred years ago in France a butler worked for a wealthy family. He knew where the family kept all their money, hidden in a vault underneath their chateau. The butler methodically plotted to kill everyone in

the family and steal the money. One night when everyone was asleep, he crept into the house and first murdered the father and mother. Then one by one he began to murder the children. The youngest escaped because he heard noises and could not sleep. When he realized what was happening he quietly slipped out of his bedroom and hid in a closet under a pile of clothes.

For years the boy wandered the streets as an orphan. He eventually entered the seminary and became a priest. After several years he was assigned to Devil's Island as a chaplain. One afternoon one of the convict inmates came running in from the fields, frantically calling for the chaplain. "There is a man dying out in the field, Father. Come quickly."

The priest ran out with the inmate and reached the dying prisoner. Kneeling down beside him, the priest lifted the man's head onto his lap and asked if he would like to confess his sins. The dying man refused. "Why, my son?" asked the priest. "Because God will never forgive me for what I have done. I could never be acceptable to God."

"But what have you done that is so bad?" the priest continued. And the man went on to tell the story of how he had killed the whole family for whom he had worked so that he could have their money. Only a little boy escaped because he could not find him.

Then the priest said to the dying man, "If I can forgive and accept you then certainly God can forgive you. And I forgive you from my heart. It was my family you killed, and I am that little boy."

The convict cried and told the priest how he had been haunted all his life over what he had done, though no one else knew about it. Even the authorities never found out. The two men cried together. As the priest was giving the dying man absolution, the prisoner died with his head resting on the priest's lap.

This powerful story, which I have heard in other places and know to be true, speaks clearly of the great compassion and love which God has for us, no matter what has happened or when it occurred. God accepts us totally; we, in turn, are challenged to accept others, especially those who might appear to be unacceptable.

2. A story is told of the famous artist Leonardo da Vinci. When he had completed his masterpiece, the "Mona Lisa," he went to a nearby tavern to celebrate the event with his friends. While in conversation and sipping a little of the local wine, Leonardo noticed that many in the tavern were making sport of an ugly fool who made his living going from tavern to tavern, entertaining patrons for a spare coin or a crust of bread. This man truly was an ugly person; he seemed to be more a troll than a man. His small beady eyes were not centered in his oversized head. His ears were like cauliflower and his nose was as large as a gourd, with an ugly mole on its tip. His mouth and jaw were locked in a perpetual grimace.

As those in the tavern continued to mock the fool, a contentious rival artist hurled a challenge to the great da Vinci. "You are a master," said the man. "Can you make in paint a beauty of this ugly fool?" Leonardo could not avoid the challenge, for to do so would forever place him in doubt with his followers. "Why not?" responded Leonardo. "If I can paint the most beautiful woman in the world in my Mona Lisa then I can certainly make an Adonis of this ugly fool. Return here tonight at the call of vespers and I will reveal the work I have done." Leonardo had little time, far less than normal for such a project, so he began in earnest.

Several hours later the bell in the cathedral church rang for vespers and the crowd began to assemble at the tavern. It was filled to overflowing; it seemed that the whole city of Florence had heard the challenge and had come to see what the master had accomplished. Leonardo stood before his new painting, which was covered by a curtain, and called for quiet. Patrons continued to murmur — What would the painting reveal? Would the fool's eyes now be blue and centered in his face? Would his nose be noble and Roman? Would his lips be gentle but firm? Would his large ears now be petite and soft? When the noise subsided Leonardo called out, "Behold my masterpiece!" He slowly withdrew the curtain to reveal his work; the crowd held its breath. The painting was an exact image of the ugly fool — not one hair or expression was out of place. The silence in the tavern was deafening. The rival artist cried out, "The ugly fool was too much of a challenge, even for the great Leonardo da Vinci." "Not so," responded Leonardo. Then, pointing to the face of the fool, he said, "This face was painted by the hand of God and only a fool would dare presume to change or replace the work of the Master." Leonardo da Vinci had used a fool to shame the proud. If we are not careful, God may do the same with us.

We often become enamored by the powerful, beautiful, and wealthy in our society. We almost naturally gravitate toward those things and people which we perceive will bring us the most fulfillment or will best meet our needs. In the parable of the wheat and tares, Jesus challenges us to think about how we treat others, the prejudices we hold, and the ways we need to be converted to a life of greater patience and tolerance.

Points Of Challenge And Questions To Ponder

1. How do we treat people who are different than us? Do we demonstrate our intolerance and impatience with family, friends, neighbors, and associates at work? This parable calls us to ponder a change of heart.

2. What are our expectations of others? Do we possess deep-seated animosity, prejudice, or feelings of resentment? Why do we feel this way?

3. Do we always want to take control of the situation and settle the issue now? Can we be patient enough to allow God to act as the Lord may dictate? What is the root of our lack of trust in the Lord?

4. Do we believe in the power of conversion in our lives and those of others? Can we give people the benefit of the doubt that God can bring about *metanoia* in them?

5. What role can we play as individuals and community in making systemic change and removing the causes and manifestations of social sin in our world? What is God's call in our lives as the Lord's disciples? God calls us to act to make the world a better place now and for those who will follow.

Exegesis And Explanation Of The Parable

The parable of the wheat and tares is, like the story of the sower (Matthew 13:1-9, 18-23), a parable combined with its allegorical interpretation. Scholars have found this passage more problematic to explain, however, because great debate exists on its origins — did it come from Jesus or is it a reshaping by the evangelist of material drawn from another source? The answer to the question leads to different interpretations as to the pericope's function in Matthew and its purpose in Jesus' teaching ministry.

Some exegetes comment that the nucleus of the parable was part of Jesus' original teaching, at least in its structure. The general portrait depicted in the parable corresponds accurately with the agricultural life in Palestine — a large estate operated by slave labor, grain fields that possess a considerable amount of weeds, and the use of weeds for fuel. If the direct source is Jesus then it appears that the parable was directed against exclusive tendencies that began to arise in the Christian community of Israel in the post-Resurrection period. The "purity" of membership in such groups as the Pharisees, Zealots, and Essenes of the Qumran community was gaining popularity among the first followers of Jesus. Zealous believers, under the banner of maintaining true teaching, were causing damage to the community by passing judgment on fellow disciples and cutting them off from the church. Jesus rejected this practice and thus the parable, in allowing wheat and tares to grow together, suggests a more open attitude toward membership. This understanding of the parable indicates that even before Jesus' death the nascent Christian community was experiencing problems with discipleship — in particular whether it should expel from its ranks those members whose lives were in some way judged as evil.

The parable understood in this way is not a call to passivity, but rather an exhortation to patience. Jesus is not suggesting that his followers should ignore injustice, violence, or other wrongs of society that evil brings, but rather is reminding the disciples that they do not have the ability to rid the world of all its "weeds." Sometimes attempts to remove weeds cause more harm than good. The parable says, however, that evil is temporary and that the weeds will ultimately be destroyed. In an imperfect world we are given the task of living as faithfully and as obediently as possible, confident in the end that the harvest will be pure, differentiating between the good and the bad. People should not take vengeance, but leave such action to God.

Biblical scholars have produced considerable evidence that suggests the parable was not spoken by Jesus. A threefold development of the parable and its allegory has been suggested. First, Mark's parable of the farmer and the growing seed (4:26-29) was written. Next, Matthew amplified the detail and specified the application of Jesus' teaching in Mark to a particular problem present in the community to which the evangelist wrote (generally believed to be Aramaic-speaking converts in Palestine). Last, Matthew added an allegorical interpretation with emphasis on judgment, an issue not in question in the original parable.

The parable itself (verses 24-30), however, poses a difficulty in the unrealistic situations it presents, leading many exegetes to conclude the passage was at least reshaped and possibly totally written by Matthew. First, it was common practice in Palestine to root out darnel (most probably the weed in question) while crops were growing, even more than once. Thus, the landowner's direction was a departure from standard practice. Next, the setting in the passage is a large plantation operated by slave labor, yet the owner sows the seed and "reapers" conduct the harvest. The specific introduction of weeds is not necessary since weeds appear on their own with any operation of sowing. Moreover, the whole scenario with the "enemy" and the "slaves" appears to have been artifically created to prepare for the later interpretation which will attribute the presence of bad people among the good in the church to the activity of Satan. A contrived situation is also apparent in the idea of intentionally sowing weeds, since a process of gathering weed-seed separately would be painstaking at best. Additionally, slaves who worked fields and their landowners would have understood that weeds were natural. There would thus be no need to conclude immediately that an "enemy" was at work.

The allegorical interpretation of the parable, verses 36-43, is most certainly a creation of the evangelist. In the parable, whether it has its origins in Jesus or Matthew, emphasis is placed on patience and tolerance, yet the interpretation makes no reference to these issues. Rather, this allegory applies the original parable to the contemporary church to whom Matthew wrote. The risen Christ sows good seed (people) who establish the church, while Satan sows evil. The evangelist appears to be very disturbed with the mixed state of the church, which contains many who enthusiastically call "Lord, Lord" but refuse to follow the Master's teaching. Matthew's interpretation assures him and his readers that a day of reckoning will come for these "pseudo" disciples. In short order the glorified Christ will send his angels to purify the church and root out and destroy those who disregard the Lord's moral teaching. Thus, the interpretation changes the meaning of the original parable by failing to allegorize the issues of patience and tolerance.

Matthew's interpretation stresses the eschatological dimension of Jesus' teaching. In many ways this passage may be accurately called the allegory of the harvest where the children of the kingdom and the children of the evil one will be separated and judged. Some scholars suggest that this passage is a prelude to the rest of the chapter and to the evangelist's famous judgment parable in chapter 25.

The interpretation poses a second problem in its understanding of evil. In attributing the presence of tares and the evil they bring to an outside enemy, the evangelist is using a theological consideration uncommon to Jesus in the Synoptics. Verses 36-43 give the impression that there are two kinds of people in the world — good and bad — and that all remain in the state they were created. Humans are not seen as individuals with personal characters who are capable of progress or degeneration, but as people belonging to two classes according to their origins. This contradicts the idea that God created all things good and Satan later corrupted some people. It also disagrees with other parables (and the general message of Scripture) which speak of the inclusive nature of the kingdom. This inconsistency gives more evidence to the idea that Matthew reshaped the parable and its interpretation to his needs, in his great fear of outside influences present in the Gentile church.

Context Of The Parable

Context In The Church Year

The parable of the wheat and tares, as with all the parables of Jesus, presents us with a challenge in daily life. Pentecost or Ordinary Time is the church's opportunity to encourage the Christian community to take the multiple lessons of Scripture, one by one, and apply them to our lives of faith. This parable gives us the twofold challenge of being patient and tolerant, but with the consolation that in the end God will triumph over evil. Following the parable of the sower, this passage continues the church's presentation of the parables in Matthew, chapter 13. Next week the last parable in this chapter will be presented before the church returns to more direct teaching by Jesus on the rule of life.

Context With Other Gospels

The parable of the wheat and tares is exclusive to Matthew's Gospel, although some parallels to other inspired writings exist. The connection between this pericope and Mark 4:26-29 has been explored above. While some images are consistent, any significant link between these passages can only be explained through a radical reshaping of Mark's original account. This parable is contained in the apocryphal Gospel of Thomas (57) in summary fashion. The fact that Thomas does not have an allegorical interpretation of this parable provides further evidence that verses 36-43 of Matthew's account do not come from Jesus.

Context With First And Second Lessons

First Lesson: Isaiah 44:6-8 or Wisdom 12:13, 16- 19. Wisdom literature provides many sources of inspiration for its readers today. In this passage the author speaks of how God cares for people in the Lord's quest for justice for all. The clemency and leniency of God are stressed by the author; there are always grounds for hope that repentance will be received for our transgressions.

This passage connects well with the eschatological aspects of the parable of the wheat and tares. God will judge justly those who have persevered in their lives of trial among the weeds of the world.

There is no need for humans to become impatient with the world; God knows the situation and has the right plan for the harvest. What is necessary is human patience and a sense of persistence in walking the road with the Lord.

Second Lesson: Romans 8:12-25. Often people say, "Lord, give me patience and give it to me now!" I suspect that Paul might have used this adage for himself and his dealings with the Romans. He uses the image of human desire to illustrate our need for patience. Creation, especially God's greatest creation, the human race, waits for God. We wait in hope and we wait with patience. We want things now, but time is necessary. Paul wants the Romans to know of the need to be patient and to persevere in all that they do.

People often become frustrated when they do not obtain what they want in the time frame that they deem appropriate or correct. God, however, does not work on the human clock nor under the constraint of human necessity. We must do our best to understand the need for patience, that waiting can assist us, even though at the time we would never believe that such was true. Waiting allows us to be honed and fire-tried and thus made ready for the challenges that God will give us. Paul's exhortation to the Romans must be our lesson as well.

---

1. Joseph F. Girzone, *Joshua and the Children* (New York: Macmillan), pp. 9-10.

75

Chapter 6

Finding Christ:
The Treasure Of A Lifetime

Matthew 13:44-52

"The kingdom of heaven is like treasure hidden in a field, which someone found and hid; then in his joy he goes and sells all that he has and buys that field.

"Again, the kingdom of heaven is like a merchant in search of fine pearls; on finding one pearl of great value, he went and sold all that he had and bought it.

"Again, the kingdom of heaven is like a net that was thrown into the sea and caught fish of every kind; when it was full, they drew it ashore, sat down, and put the good into baskets but threw out the bad. So it will be at the end of the age. The angels will come out and separate the evil from the righteous and throw them into the furnace of fire, where there will be weeping and gnashing of teeth.

"Have you understood all this?" They answered, "Yes." And he said to them, "Therefore every scribe who has been trained for the kingdom of heaven is like the master of a household who brings out of his treasure what is new and what is old."

Theme

Along the road of life we will make many discoveries. We will find an occupation to exercise our skills, a place to live that meets our needs and desires, possibly a spouse who helps us live life more fully, and ultimately a sense of fulfillment in our day-to-day Christian walk. The greatest prize, however, the one we must sell all possessions, opportunities, and possibilities in order to receive, is Jesus. We will only keep this greatest of all treasures if we are committed and surrender ourselves to the Lord's will. The buried treasure and pearl of great price are ours for the asking, but without commitment they soon will be lost. Our priority must be for Jesus and his message of love and peace for all people.

Spiritual Food For The Journey

Searching for the special prize of life, however one may define it, is a quest in which all people participate. Children often save their allowance and the money they make through odd jobs to purchase the one item they "have always wanted." They are willing to sacrifice time, resources, and opportunity for the one thing they feel they must have. Couples in love often take extraordinary chances or do unheard-of things for the one whom they feel will bring them the special happiness we all seek. Great athletes, like those who compete in the Olympics, focus years of their lives on the one opportunity to compete against the world's best in any one sport or event, and the chance to win the coveted gold medal. Parents will deny themselves certain items and place all extra money in a fund so that one day their children can attend college and have that much more of an opportunity to make a significant contribution to our society.

Contemporary life promotes the material world or the people in it as the treasure of life, but for us who bear the name Christian another answer must be found. We are almost programmed today to believe that what we need must be measurable, observable, or tangible; there is no significant thought of the invisible, intangible, or supernatural as a goal for which we would sacrifice and give all we possess. Yet, the ultimate goal for the Christian is to find God and to live in the Lord's presence forever. Although this aim is not recognizable by most, it is the only objective that will bring us home and lead us to eternal life.

We need to discover or rediscover Jesus in our lives. There are so many things that demand our time, resources, and talent that we seldom have the opportunity to concentrate on the things that really matter in life. The parables of the buried treasure, pearl of great price, and dragnet teach us that we need God. We may be actively seeking the Lord or we may be wandering, but when we find Jesus we must be willing to give up all and surrender ourselves to obtain the eternal life he offers to us. We may encounter the Lord at a time of spiritual ecstasy or in the depths of despair. We must, therefore, be ready to pay the price and not allow God's presence to pass us by. God will come knocking, but are we listening? God seeks entrance, but are we ready to open the door? The answer is ours.

Application Of The Parable To Contemporary Life

Sermon Openings
1. When she was a little girl her parents bought a cottage by the lake. It was a small and humble place, but it soon would be filled with many memories. Each summer the family went to the lake. She and her brother and sisters swam in the lake almost everyday. On special occasions her father rented a boat and the whole family paddled around the lake. She learned how to fish and even tried her hand at water skiing. Vacations were a constant source of joy because of the little cottage by the lake.

When she grew a little older and entered high school other interests were found besides the cottage by the lake. Clothes, parties, and especially boys occupied the majority of her time. She went to summer school to improve her mind, but also to enhance her social life. The few times that she did go to the lake were with friends. Horseplay, long walks along the shore of the lake, and roasting marshmallows over a dying campfire were memories she collected.

As time passed she graduated from high school, went to college, and got a job. She became successful and married the man of her dreams. She was far too busy to go to the little cottage by the lake. Even when her parents died and left the house to her she could not muster the energy or resolve to go to the lake; it no longer seemed to fit her taste. After all, it was small and inconvenient due to its location; it would take lots of remodeling to satisfy her tastes.

The lake was more like a big pond; it was hardly something of which to be proud. When she had children they convinced her to go to the lake a couple of times, but her attitude rubbed off on them and no one had a good time. In the end she abandoned the cottage completely. She was a successful businesswoman who lectured and traveled widely and thus did not have any time for the cottage. Besides, she had all that was needed, a fancy car, designer clothes, and a palatial home.

One day while at work she received a message from her secretary. Vandals had broken into the little cottage by the lake and burned it to the ground. Loss of the cottage didn't matter to her, but for some strange reason she felt compelled to go to the lake. When she arrived she stood in the ashes of what once was the little cottage by the lake. Surrounded by the charred rubble, she remembered and began to cry uncontrollably; she couldn't stop. At that moment she came to a stunning revelation. If all the fancy things she had — the car, designer clothes, palatial home — were lost she would not cry as hard as she was now for the little cottage by the lake. The place had become part of her and she never realized it. That day when she left, the lake looked bigger than it ever had before. Her tears had made it so.[1]

What is truly important in our lives? What occupies our time, energy, thoughts, and resources? What value do we place on the various things of our lives — our opportunities, our health, our material possessions, our relationship with God? In today's Gospel passage we hear several short vignettes, images of the kingdom of God, which tell us that there is nothing more important than our relationship with the Lord.

2. "Late have I loved you, O Beauty so ancient and so new, late have I loved you." This famous line comes from an equally famous book. It was written after a life of trial, searching, and change. It was written by a man who had found conversion in his life. He was born in the city of Thagaste, now in the country of Algeria, in the year 354. His father was Patricius, a Roman citizen and pagan. His mother was Monica, a prayerful Christian woman of simple means.

As a youth he was an intelligent, questioning boy. Yet, he seemed to live his life as an individual; he was quite self-centered. All of life was for him — his projects, his education, his welfare. As a young man he was a teacher of rhetoric. He became well-known for his intelligence and probing mind. As a young adult he was involved in a relationship and fathered a son, Adeodatus.

Despite his fame and success, his life of "individualism" lacked something. The void he felt was community; he needed the presence of others and he needed God. Thus, he began to search for that which was missing in his life, his need for community and God. Pagan religions offered no help to this probing mind. Manichaeism, a semi-Christian heretical movement, attracted him, but after a few years his dissatisfaction returned. Finally, this man of speech and debate answered the call to Christianity. He found people; he found community; he found God. He learned that the world was not *me*; the world is *us*!

"Late have I loved you, O Beauty so ancient and so new." These words are found in the *Confessions*, the autobiography of Saint Augustine, bishop of Hippo, one of the most gifted and famous men who ever lived. Augustine was a man who experienced the call to conversion and change in his life. He was a man who searched and ultimately found God.

Points Of Challenge And Questions To Ponder

1. What is truly important for us? How do we order our priorities and where does the search for God fall? Nothing must impede us from our goal of finding God.

2. Are we constantly looking for God or is the Lord placed on "the back burner" in our day-to-day lives? Where do we look for God? Do we limit our search?

3. What do you need to live? Are we attached to the world or do we place our lot with God? Who or what has our loyalty?

4. What are we willing to sacrifice in order to find our way home to God? What things, people, or ideas impede our progress in moving toward the Lord?

5. Do we listen to the call of the Lord? Do we make time each day to talk with God? Do we give ourselves the opportunity to encounter God or have we shut the door to the Lord's invitation to life?

Exegesis And Explanation Of The Parable

The triad of parables contained in Matthew 13:44-52 concludes Jesus' discourse in this section of the Gospel and tells the reader that all the previous teachings will become more meaningful when we truly discover the Lord. Matthew uses the parables of the buried treasure, pearl of great price, and dragnet in the lake to instruct his readers in their need for Christ. True disciples must be willing to dispossess themselves of all things when they discover Jesus and his message of love. In this pericope Jesus addresses his chosen apostles as examples of all disciples who must surrender themselves to Christ's unique mission and demonstrate their commitment to the new way. Israel as a nation is called by Jesus to give up all it hoped for or gained by struggle if it stands in the way of the message received in finding Christ, the greatest of all treasures.

The parables of buried treasure and the great pearl provide some similarities in their common message of discovering the Kingdom of Heaven. Both parables deal with the great joy of the Kingdom of Heaven and the need for true disciples to exhibit complete self-surrender to Jesus' will and teaching. In both cases the one who discovers is filled with joy in what is found and is willing to sell all in order to claim the great prize. Overwhelming joy at the find allows them no other action but to sell all to gain the new reward. The sense of fulfillment attained by the man in the field and the merchant through their independent discoveries will never again be equaled.

The parables demonstrate in similar ways how the Kingdom has its effect on the world through the decision and action of the individual. The treasure and the pearl are the source of power that gives rise to actions of people. Thus, the manifestations of God's Kingdom lead to action on the part of the individual. Each person who discovers the great prize can sell all or keep what is already possessed. Emphasis is placed in each parable on the discovery, whether accidental in the case of the treasure or as a result of a diligent search by the pearl merchant. Once the great prize is found a decision must be made on what will be done. Since both people sell all to possess their new discovery, the parables stand as exhortations for us to do likewise.

These parables should not be misconstrued as teaching that the Kingdom of Heaven is an individual possession that must be earned through the renunciation of material things. The central idea is that God's Kingdom is something that is to be received as a gift. It is not something that can be acquired and held as a legal and permanent possession. Yet, one cannot be passive, as represented by the parable of the farmer and the growing seed (Mark 4:26-29), but must actively seek the great prize which is discovered. Those whose eyes have been opened by what they have found must commit themselves wholeheartedly in faith and obedience to Jesus' teaching.

The early church fathers, such as Irenaeus and Augustine, held an interesting perspective on these two parables. For them the treasure and pearl were Christ. Converts who found Christ gave up everything in their old lifestyles and devoted themselves totally to Jesus. Christ is thus the treasure or pearl along life's highway. Some travelers are wandering (the man in the field) and others are seeking (the merchant), but when either finds Jesus the response is total self-surrender. They joyfully sell all in order to have Christ.

The parables of buried treasure and pearl of great price formed a unitive message for those who heard them the first time. In both cases the ones who discover these great treasures take a risk in their common decision to sell all for the one great reward. If a person can take a chance on an unknown treasure and a shrewd merchant is able to renounce all for the purchase of one great pearl, how much more highly should the disciples of Jesus be willing to abandon everything that is possessed in order to secure the one item that is necessary for eternal life.

The parable of the dragnet shows a clear connection to the parable of wheat and tares (Matthew 13:24-30, 36-43). The actual parable, verses 47 and 48, speaks of how a net catches good and worthless things, fish and other items. Thus, as with the weeds, the Kingdom of Heaven is depicted as a mixture of good and evil. The interpretation, verses 49 and 50, again like the eschatologically-oriented allegory of the wheat and tares, can be seen as an instruction not to separate people in order to create a "pure" church. Thus, a warning is given against any impatience that would lead Jesus' disciples in their own right to execute the judgment of God. If the net represents the preaching of the gospel, then Jesus' message is clearly directed to all people without discrimination. Followers of Jesus are to go about their daily tasks, witness to fellow disciples, whomever they be, bring them together in the church, instruct them in their need for faith and repentance, and direct their attention to judgment, when the final separation of the wicked and righteous will take place.

Scholars are united in their belief that verses 49 and 50 are an allegorical interpretation of the basic parable. In certain ways, however, this interpretation is out of context with the situation presented in the story of the dragnet. Taking a page from apocalyptic literature, the evangelist has angels separate the evil from the good, with the former sent to be burned. Fish that were not useful would have been thrown back into the lake or used as fertilizer for crops; they would not have been burned. The allegory is also flawed in its absence of specified meaning for the net, the sea, and the basket which holds the fish. Most exegetes believe that Matthew uses allegory to refer to the church and its "mixed" status. As with the parable of the wheat and tares, the task of separation is not that of humans, but belongs solely with God. This understanding suggests that separation of good from evil is the central point of the parable, the gathering of people by the net of Jesus' preaching. Thus, Christians are not predestined to be chosen for eternal life, but they must persevere in doing what Jesus taught.

Many scholars, on the other hand, believe that verse 47 alone was the original parable. In this case the theme of inclusivity is even more prominent, but the idea of judgment is absent. Scholars point to the fact that it is the fishing and not the sorting which is of primary importance. As the fisherman spreads a net to capture every kind of fish before sorting, so the Kingdom of God embraces every human. This universal appeal, seen in the experience of the Apostolic Church, would have been justification for the mission to the Gentiles. Additionally, such an interpretation says that the gospel makes no discrimination of rank, class, wealth or poverty, trade or profession. The grace of God is offered freely to all.

Matthew concludes this section of his Gospel with an instruction on what is necessary for disciples who hear the previous words of Jesus. The evangelist sees the disciples as prototypes of the teacher of the Law who becomes a disciple in the kingdom of heaven. He says that the true teacher of the Law has learned from Jesus both the old and the new — God's Law from the Hebrew Scriptures and its new interpretation proclaimed by Jesus and realized in all that he does. Some have suggested the old and new is Jesus' own teaching and its new interpretation in the discussions of the contemporary community of disciples. In either case, it appears certain that for Matthew the whole collection of parables in chapter 13 is a didactic discourse on the Kingdom of God. Teachers in this new way are disciples who remain learners, open to the new, throughout their lives.

This conclusion also serves as an important appendix to the parables presented previously. Ordinary Christians have direct access to the mysteries of the Kingdom of Heaven as revealed through the parables and other teachings of Jesus, but they require the assistance of scribes and others learned in the tradition who can help them appropriate the wisdom of the Hebrew Scriptures to their understanding of what God is doing in the post-resurrection church. Matthew stresses the new teaching of Jesus as the path that must be followed.

Many Scripture exegetes believe that verse 52 is Matthew's self-portrait, or at least how he conceived his mission as an evangelist. His comparison with a householder suggests that he held a position of authority in the community of disciples, but his office was to disseminate the message to other members of the household. He has at his disposal a treasure — the old and new. Figuratively, these represent the stores of knowledge which the evangelist has accumulated. Matthew believed himself to be a disciple who learned the mystery of the Kingdom of Heaven from Jesus. Now as an experienced scribe in the Jewish tradition, the evangelist must make his contribution to the growth of the tradition by applying the teaching of Jesus to a variety of emerging situations. He sees the Christian scribe as versed in the Law of Moses and in the Law of Christ, which is the fulfillment, not the abolition, of the ancient Law. Matthew understands himself as an interpreter, guardian, and dispenser of the tradition.

Context Of The Parable

Context In The Church Year
The three parables of the treasure, pearl, and dragnet in the sea form the end of our reading of chapter 13 in Matthew. For the past three weeks the church has used the parables of this highly significant chapter to instruct us in the need for perseverance, patience, inclusivity, and the need to think carefully about what is truly important in our lives. Parables were used by Jesus to be instructive, and they can be used by us today for a similar purpose. While scholars debate the various intricacies of these special stories of the Lord, the faithful can use the teachings in their daily lives. The church will continue with its semi-continuous reading of Matthew's Gospel throughout the "A" liturgical year, but the teaching of Jesus in parable form will not be re-introduced until Pentecost week seventeen.

Context With Other Gospels
The parables in this section of Matthew's Gospel have parallels in the apocryphal Gospel of Thomas. The parables of the treasure and pearl are found in Thomas, 109 and 76 respectively, but with different emphases. The story of the treasure is a comment on an opportunity missed. A son sells the land he has inherited

without realizing that his father hid a treasure on it. In the case of the pearl, the merchant sells all and buys the one pearl because it suits his fancy. The appearance of these two parables as separate pericopes in Thomas suggests that the parables may not have been originally proclaimed together by Jesus, but rather were joined by Matthew. The parable of the dragnet, found in the Gospel of Thomas 8, also presents a different perspective — the fisherman throws away all the little fish and keeps only a single large one.

This triad of parables is unique to Matthew, although some parallels in theme are present in other parts of the Canon of Scripture. The parables of the treasure and the pearl exhibit the language of Wisdom literature where wisdom is referred to as a treasure (Proverbs 2:4, 8:18-24, Isaiah 33:6) and as a pearl (Proverbs 3:14-15, 8:11 and Job 28:17-18). The image of the fish net is used by Mark (1:16) and Luke (5:4-7) but involves the use of boats and crews; it is not used by one man.

Context With First And Second Lessons
First Lesson: 1 Kings 3:5-12. Solomon is known through the tradition as a man of great wisdom. This passage from 1 Kings tells us that Solomon had the opportunity to ask God for anything, but he chose "an understanding mind to govern ... [to] discern between good and evil...." Solomon possessed the insight of what was truly important in life. While riches and power might have been helpful to him as a king, he chose what would be permanent in order to bring the most benefit for the people whom God had given him to shepherd. Solomon's ability to choose wisely was rewarded by God. In opting for that which only God can give, Solomon chose what he needed to govern and also to be in union with God.

Second Lesson: Romans 8:26-39. Paul writes to the Christian community at Rome about what God will do for those who make the right choices. Disciples of Jesus, those who truly love him, will be called, justified, and glorified. When we find Jesus and take his message into our hearts we have the greatest of all prizes, the treasure of a lifetime, the pearl of great price. If we sell all, place our hope and faith in him, and persevere in our daily tasks, then we will find the eternal life we seek. God's promise as articulated by Saint Paul is irrevocable.

---

1. Paraphrased from "The Lady of the Lake," in John R. Aurelio, *Colors! Stories of the Kingdom* (New York: The Crossroad Publishng Company, 1993), pp. 40-41.

Chapter 7

Sharing God's Unlimited Forgiveness With Others

Matthew 18:21-35

Then Peter came and said to him, "Lord if another member of the church sins against me, how often should I forgive? As many as seven times?" Jesus said to him, "Not seven times, but, I tell you, seventy-seven times.

"For this reason the kingdom of heaven can be compared to a king who wished to settle accounts with his slaves. When he began the reckoning, one who owed him ten thousand talents was brought to him; and, as he could not pay, his lord ordered him to be sold, together with his wife and children and all his possessions, and payment to be made. So the slave fell on his knees before him, saying, 'Have patience with me, and I will pay you everything.' And out of pity for him, the lord of the slave released him and forgave him the debt. But that same slave, as he went out, came upon one of his fellow slaves who owed him a hundred denarii; and seizing him by the throat, he said, 'Pay what you owe.' Then his fellow slave fell down and pleaded with him, 'Have patience with me, and I will pay you.' But he refused; then he went and threw him into prison until he would pay the debt. When his fellow slaves saw what had happened, they were greatly distressed, and they went and reported to their lord all that had taken place. Then his lord summoned him and said to him, 'You wicked slave! I forgave you all that debt because you pleaded with me. Should you not have had mercy on your fellow slave, as I had mercy on you?'

*And in anger his lord handed him over to be tortured
until he would pay his entire debt. So my heavenly father
will also do to every one of you, if you do not forgive your
brother or sister from your heart."*

Theme

Forgiveness is a virtue in short supply these days. Contemporary society tells us that one's pride cannot expose the humility needed to express sorrow for what one has done. Similarly, many of us hold grudges and deep hurts from the past and we refuse to let go. True forgiveness means that we leave all our pre-held prejudices, hurts, and indiscretions behind and move on to a new relationship with God and God's people. God willingly and without price forgives anyone who seeks reunion with him. God was the one who first loved us and asks us to love in return. In a similar way, God's unlimited forgiveness to us must be shared without reservation or need for return. We must forgive as God has forgiven us.

Spiritual Food For The Journey

Reconciliation is the concept of being reunited, of taking what is fractured and again making it whole. God created us in an imperfect, incomplete, and broken state. Thus, there is never a time that a human does not need reconciliation to bind up what has been scattered in our lives, whether that be people, promises, commitments, injuries of the heart or mind, or broken dreams.

Reconciliation is a process, like life itself, and it cannot be experienced completely unless the pattern is followed. First, we must become reconciled with ourselves. If we cannot believe that we are good, holy, and worthy of God's grace, then we will never fully understand our need to seek God. It is not easy to forgive oneself, but it is an essential first step. Next, we need to forgive and be forgiven by our neighbor. Life brings so much heartache in relationships with others. Sometimes the pain is great and felt very deeply. Reconciliation is required to reverse trends toward estrangement which make pain persist. We need to be vulnerable to recognize our own faults and allow others to know that we realize our guilt. Concurrently we must be compassionate enough to allow others to humble themselves before us and ask our forgiveness. Once we have forgiven ourselves and one another, then we are ready to accept the magnificent and unlimited forgiveness of God.

Reconciliation is absolutely essential to the Christian life. The incompleteness of humanity naturally seeks wholeness and healing, things that can ultimately only be found in an ongoing and growing relationship with God. Mercy and judgment are the prerogatives of God and they are exercised now and at the hour of our death and judgment. Let us accept God's unlimited forgiveness and in turn demonstrate like action toward our brothers and sisters in Christ.

Application Of The Parable To Contemporary Life

Sermon Openings
1. Webster's Dictionary defines the concept of equilibrium as a static or dynamic state of balance between opposing forces or actions. There are many examples of equilibrium around us that are so obvious we never give them a second thought. For example, here I am standing before you. Why don't I sink into the floor? Why am I not floating in the air? You probably will answer: well, that is obvious, I am standing on the floor and the floor is supporting me. This is certainly true. Science tells us, however, that the process is a bit more complicated. Physicists say that the floor pushes up on my feet as much as and in the opposite direction of my weight or mass which pushes down. Thus, I am not moving up or down; I am in a state of equilibrium.

What about all of you? The process of equilibrium can be applied to you as well. You are all able to sit, without falling, without floating in the air, because the pew upon which you are sitting pushes up to support your weight which pushes down.

There are many other examples of equilibrium which we could mention. We know that oil and water do not mix; the oil will rest on top of the water. Why is this? It is because the oil is less dense.

This is the state of equilibrium between oil and water. However, if we were to dissolve some sugar in the oil and water combination the equilibrium would change. Try it some time; see what happens. If we squeeze a rubber ball we see it compress; if we let go it will expand. Equal and opposite forces keep the ball in a state of equilibrium.

If we lose our state of equilibrium we have problems. If we walk on soft ground or mud we begin to sink. If we sit on an unstable chair or bench we may fall. If we squeeze something too hard, it will not regain its former shape.

One might ask, why all this talk of equilibrium? I think equilibrium is a good way of describing the concepts of forgiveness and reconciliation of which our Gospel passage speaks this day. Clearly we hear that forgiveness must be kept in balance or equilibrium in order to be effective. We need to forgive others as God has forgiven us.

2. Have you ever taken a course of action or held a particular attitude, all the while thinking that it was correct and then never giving it another thought? That is what happened with Ludovico Gadda, Pope Leo XIV. Ludovico was born in a small Italian town, like many of the popes, all from Italy, who have occupied the Chair of Saint Peter since the time of the Council of Trent in the sixteenth century. It seemed that Ludovico was destined for ministry and priesthood from his earliest days. He was ordained and lived a very traditional life as a parish priest. He lived by the canons and doctrines of the faith. Ludovico was good at what he did. Thus, he was made bishop of the diocese. Later he was moved to a larger metropolitan area and was made archbishop. Still later he was made a cardinal and finally he was elected Pope. The people in Ludovico's hometown were not that surprised by the course of events.

Upon assuming the Chair of Peter, Ludovico, who took the name of Leo XIV, was invested with much power and authority. The power he held was beneficial to some but it was highly detrimental to others. Like all of us, the Pope had an agenda. He took a course of action; he held certain attitudes and opinions. The problem was that he never reflected on his actions and attitudes. He never considered the possibility that he was hurting others by what he did or thought.

What would it take for him to change? For Ludovico it would be a bout with serious illness. Chest pains landed the Pope in the hospital. Doctors told him he needed heart bypass surgery. The thought of such major surgery placed the Pope in a more contemplative mood. He began to think about his life and what he had done. He began to realize that he might have hurt others. He knew that he needed to change, to find healing, forgiveness, and reconciliation. But for Pope Leo XIV it would be too late. His inability to look into his heart would prove fatal. He would be assassinated by the very people he had hurt before he had the opportunity to change his ways.

So goes in summary the last of Morris West's trilogy of novels which describes popes and faith. The name of the book is *Lazarus*. Morris West's tale is a good example of what our Gospel describes — namely, that we need to look into out hearts, see if wrong has been done, and then seek forgiveness and reconciliation if needed.

Points Of Challenge And Questions To Ponder

1. Can we humble ourselves before the Lord and God's people to seek forgiveness? Do we realize our absolute need for God's mercy in order to gain wholeness?

2. Do we hold deep-seated and painful prejudices against others? Do we have the ability to leave our past baggage at the front door as we enter into a new realm of mercy and forgiveness? Can we move out of the past into the future?

3. Are we too proud to allow others to gain access to us? Do we keep barriers of past experience in place so that others may not cross and find the wholeness, the reconciliation they seek with us?

4. Do we break the chain of reconciliation at some stage? Can we forgive ourselves and others? Will we allow ourselves to give and accept forgiveness?

5. Many times we seek God's forgiveness for what we have done. We are truly penitent in our cry. But are we in sufficient balance to realize our need to forgive others from our hearts?

Exegesis And Explanation Of The Parable

Matthew 18:21-35 is divided into two sections: a question and response, and a parable of unlimited forgiveness that demonstrates God's munificence and our need to respond. In verses 21 and 22 Peter asks the Lord how often he must forgive when one sins. Behind this inquiry are two possible concerns, one that focuses on the offended party and the other on the offender. Human experience suggests that there is a limit to patience with misbehavior. Peter may be asking Jesus: If one insults me repeatedly, must I continue suffering the indignity? He may also be asking: Is it in the best interests of my brother or sister for me to tolerate such actions when it is clear that repentance is superficial and there is no intent to change?

Jesus' response to Peter addresses neither issue, but rather transposes the problem from the sphere of an ordinary relationship to another realm. The Lord's response provides the theological grounding for unlimited forgiveness. Jesus speaks of infinity in his answer to how often one must forgive. In Jewish tradition the numbers seven and ten represented completion. Thus, Jesus is saying that one must be forgiving as the result of completion times completion plus completion — an infinite number of times. Certainly the 77 times is an allusion to Genesis 4:24 where Lamech boasts that he will avenge anyone 77 times who dares attack him. Thus, at this point forgiveness is juxtaposed to revenge. Followers of Jesus are thus exhorted to renounce the very human intention of "getting even" with someone who specifically injures them.

The actual parable, verses 23 to 35, has been identified by many biblical scholars as a story derived from Oriental (thus Gentile) images, a method used to contrast sharply Christian attitudes with those of pagans. In three parts the Eastern parable describes how a sultan handles accounts with his administrative officials. An audit discovers that one official, possibly a satrap from a wealthy province, has embezzled an immense amount. Because restitution is impossible, due to the size of the debt, the sultan orders that the offender be sold, along with his family, into slavery, a punishment more demeaning than execution. After the official pleads for mercy, however, the sultan reverses himself and sets the scoundrel free. In the second part of the story the official is now a creditor, not a debtor. A fellow administrator is delinquent in a small loan, one that is payable — a highly significant detail in the tale. The pardoned embezzler stands on his rights and will tolerate no breach to the contract, even with the minor official's plea. In the last scene other officials, appalled at the embezzler's treatment of his fellow administrator, report the whole incident. In his anger the sultan again changes his mind and turns the embezzler over to the torturers.

The vivid scene depicted by Matthew accentuates the contrast between God's infinite love and mercy and human impatience and unwillingness to forgive. Jesus uses the parable to tell Peter something very important about the magnitude of God's forgiving love toward sinful humans. Human iniquity is beyond the numerical count of 77, and thus God's mercy must be infinitely greater. The depth of God's mercy simply cannot be measured.

Scripture exegetes today emphasize that this parable was proclaimed not to emphasize repeated forgiveness, but unlimited forgiveness, for the debt of the embezzler is so great it cannot be repaid. The sum of 10,000 talents for the first readers or hearers of the parable could be equated for Americans today to an annual corporate or state budget — a sum beyond the capability of any one person. Despite the amount, the debt is written off without condition. Clearly Matthew wants his readers to know that followers of Jesus must act in a similar way in their relationships with one another. Those who wish to be part of the Kingdom must imitate the incalculable patience and unlimited forgiveness of God.

Commentators compare the virtues of mercy and justice as they are presented in the parable. The Jews were well versed in the mandate from the Hebrew scriptures to exercise mercy and compassion. Exodus 22:25-27, which details proper practices for loans, is one illustration of mercy. Justice was expressed in a variety of ways. The demands of the Year of Jubilee, for example, were emphasized. During this year land belonging to the dispersed was returned to the original owner and people in slavery were freed. The Jew of Jesus' day realized that mercy and justice could not be treated separately; they were interrelated. It is for this reason that Jesus tells this parable of unlimited forgiveness. In the parable the embezzler could not forgive; he applied the principle of justice without mercy. Jesus teaches his followers that the exercise of mercy is not an occasional setting aside of justice, but rather, mercy and justice must be applied together.

This parable appeals to the basic nature of God. To deny the validity of the principles of mercy, forgiveness, and patience in our human affairs is to deny the nature of God and to shut ourselves off from the Creator's love. God cannot overlook an opportunity to demonstrate mercy, for any other response is contrary to his nature. God's grace and mercy are incalculable; God accepts the sinner as if no offense had been committed. Just as we cannot earn God's favor, so we need not be concerned about God's mercy; it is ever present. Yet, the Lord expects us to treat others with mercy and forgiveness as God has loved us. Only by becoming like children and placing utter dependence upon God will we be able to transcend human wisdom and find the capability to forgive like God.

This parable is understood by several scholars to be eschatological in nature. It combines an exhortation with a warning based on mercy and forgiveness. Jewish apocalyptic literature taught that God rules the world by the two measures of mercy and judgment, but at the Last Judgement God only makes use of judgment. Jesus, on the other hand, taught that the virtue of mercy was also in force at the time of the Parousia and final judgment. The basic question for readers thus was: when at the Last Judgment does God demonstrate mercy and when does he exercise judgment? Jesus answers that where God's forbearance produces a readiness to forgive, there God's mercy grants forgiveness of debts again. The one, however, who abuses God's gift of mercy faces the full severity of judgment, as if forgiveness had never been granted. The point of the parable is clear: the only hope we have for God's grace must be found in our willingness, in our own environment, to show God's spirit of forgiveness to those whose injuries against us are, by negligible compared to our own wrongs against God.

Context Of The Parable

Context In The Church Year

After seven weeks the church again returns to a parable to describe Jesus' message of mercy, forgiveness, and love. For five consecutive Sundays we will hear various parables from Matthew's Gospel that challenge us to respond to the God who first loved us. Forgiveness is basic to the Christian message; one cannot get far as a disciple without providing and receiving forgiveness. Thus, in its initiation of five consecutive parables, the theme of unlimited forgiveness is highlighted. The Golden Rule, as we all know, says we are to love God and our neighbor as ourselves. Love is dependent upon the knowledge that mercy and forgiveness are available and will be applied. How can we be confident of God's love or our ability to love or be loved by others unless we are certain that any barrier to this love can be removed? Forgiveness, reconciliation, mercy, and compassion are trademarks of the Christian life and ones that the church in its wisdom provides for us this week.

Context With Other Gospels

While the concepts of forgiveness and mercy are basic to the gospel message, this particular parable of unlimited forgiveness is unique to Matthew. In Luke 17:4 Jesus addresses his disciples as a group and tells them that they must forgive anyone who seeks repentance from them, even if it is seven times a day. Here the message of repeated forgiveness is stressed against Matthew's parable of unlimited forgiveness.

This parable concludes chapter 18 of Matthew's Gospel with a scene that says the Christian community can live on the basis of God's inconceivable grace. Not only can the community live in such a manner, it must. Matthew in the last verse underscores this admonition to the community and its alternative — destruction in the Last Judgment. Throughout the entire chapter Matthew is concerned with helping the followers of Jesus. Only when the heart has become new and all live as children can people live as true disciples of Jesus.

Context With First And Second Lessons
First Lesson: Genesis 50:15-21. The crime perpetrated by the sons of Israel against their brother Joseph was very grave. Sold into slavery, there was little chance that the young boy would survive, let alone achieve position and greatness. Yet, Joseph defeated the odds and rose to be a leader in Egypt. Most people would have held a grudge or been vengeful toward those who committed such an offense against one's person, but Joseph was no ordinary person. He demonstrated the unlimited forgiveness that Jesus would later preach in his public ministry. Joseph stands as a model of human forgiveness for all of us.

Second Lesson: Romans 14: 1-12. Saint Paul reminds the Christian community at Rome that they are on loan to the world from God. The Lord has given us the opportunity of life in order to serve God and God's people. Thus, we have a responsibility that must not be taken lightly in our day-to-day lives. In conjunction with the parable of unlimited forgiveness we should understand that mercy and compassion are integral parts of God's law and must be exercised in our lives. We cannot properly live the life given us by God unless we demonstrate unlimited forgiveness to our brothers and sisters, in imitation of Christ who died in order to give us eternal life.

Chapter 8

It's Never Too Late

Matthew 20:1-16

"For the kingdom of heaven is like a landowner who went out early in the morning to hire laborers for his vineyard. After agreeing with the laborers for the usual daily wage, he sent them into his vineyard. When he went out about nine o'clock, he saw others standing idle in the market-place; and he said to them, 'You also go to the vineyard, and I will pay you whatever is right.' So they went. When he went out again about noon and about three o'clock, he did the same. And about five o'clock he went out and found others standing around; and he said to them, 'Why are you standing here idle all day?' They said to him, 'Because no one has hired us.' He said to them, 'You also go into the vineyard.' When evening came, the owner of the vineyard said to his manager, 'Call the laborers and give them their pay, beginning with the last and then going to the first.' When those hired about five o'clock came, each of them received the usual daily wage. Now when the first came, they thought they would receive more; but each of them also received the usual daily wage. And when they received it, they grumbled against the landowner, saying, 'These last worked only one hour, and you have made them equal to us who have borne the burden of the day and the scorching heat.' But he replied to one of them, 'Friend, I am doing you no wrong; did you not agree with me for the usual daily wage? Take what belongs to you and go; I choose to give to this last the same as I give to you. Am I not allowed to do what I choose with what belongs to me? Or are you envious because I

*am generous?' So the last will be first, and the first will
be last."*

Theme

Americans are steeped in an understanding of justice based on
the democratic system of law which we enjoy in our nation. The
so-called Protestant work ethic built this nation by encouraging
hard work with the promise of reward for our labor. Justice in this
context tells us that reward is based on our own effort; those who
choose not to extend themselves in labor will not receive the compensation given to those who work longer or harder.

Human justice, as much as it has profited peoples throughout
the centuries, cannot be applied to God. God observes with different eyes and listens with different ears to the pleas of his people.
Our Creator wants us to be part of God's family. Although great
benefit can be gained by joining early, the ultimate reward will be
the same for all. What is important is to accept God's call. It is
never too late to be with God!

Spiritual Food For The Journey

In mathematics the concept of "pi" is an example of a radical.
It is a term which cannot be precisely or fully defined or known.
We all learn in grade school that pi is 3.1416.... Pi cannot be fully
known because it consists of an infinite string of numbers that come
after the decimal point. Unlike the number 100 or even 50.50 which
have a definite and very precise value, pi is not totally definable.

Placing limits on things, like the mathematical radical pi, is the
human reality. Humans can go only so far in understanding the
infinite. We have never seen or experienced anything that is infinite, and thus we can only guess at what infinity is. We know it is
big, that it goes on forever. But this can lead to confusion, because
we can only think on the finite level. When we place limits or
boundaries on things it makes life more understandable; at least
we can recognize that which we are trying to define.

God is infinite, that is what we have been taught since the time
we first began to understand what others told us. The Hebrews

believed that Yahweh was infinite, all-powerful, all-knowing, and omnipresent. Christians believe that Jesus is like the Father in all things and, therefore, is infinite. Jesus displayed compassion and love which were beyond human understanding.

Since God is infinite, how can we understand God? We make an attempt to understand God by placing limits on God. We set boundaries that God cannot exceed so as to make possible some understanding of the infinite. Theologically speaking, I suspect, there is a need to speak of God in some finite manner. Without some bounds God is unapproachable on an intellectual level.

Our propensity to place limits on the infinite can lead to problems, however, when we speak of our understanding of God. Human beings for centuries have been placing restrictions, limits, and boundaries on God. The Hebrews were a people who constantly wanted a sign that God was with them in their struggles. They were never satisfied. God wrought the plagues in Egypt, parted the Red Sea, provided water and food in the desert, and made Israel victorious in battle when they claimed the promised land. Yet, the Hebrews continued to look for signs. The limits of their faith placed restrictions on their belief in God's providence. The stories of the judges and prophets of ancient Israel describe over and over again the people's inability to believe that God truly is infinite and will never abandon his greatest creation, the human race.

People in the time of Jesus also wanted signs. God was again placed in a straightjacket, tied up, and not allowed to be infinite. The limited faith shown by the Pharisees and other "name" people of Jewish society was applied to their unbelief in Jesus. People were amazed each time Jesus performed something miraculous. It was only because people had little faith that the actions of an infinite God were so striking. As Jesus said to his followers, "If you had faith the size of a mustard seed, you could say to this mulberry tree, 'Be uprooted and planted in the sea,' and it would obey you" (Luke 17:6).

People today are still placing limits on God. It is only natural; it is the only way we can know something of God. Yet, we transfer our limitations on the concept of God to our faith. We refuse to believe that God truly can do all things. We constantly need to be reminded of Jesus' words, "For God all things are possible" (Mark 10:27b).

To believe in the infinite is a great challenge. Christianity is such a belief. To speak of God as a person, to draw a picture of God, or think of him standing before us is at best an approximation. It is the best we can do, however, and thus is important and useful. We cannot, however, hold such limitations on our faith and what God can do for us. God truly is infinite and thus capable of all things. When we speak with and listen to God in prayer, let us remember to keep the doors of possibility open. God knows our needs before we can even share them with him. Let us allow God's gift of compassion to be boundless, infinite. Let us allow God to be God, to be the source of all goodness, compassion, and love.

Application Of The Parable To Contemporary Life

Sermon Openings
1. We are all familiar with the term "late-bloomers." It refers to people who respond later in life to an invitation and manage in the end to accomplish great things. History has known some famous late-bloomers. Fortunately for us, early or late they followed the special invitation offered by God.

Anton Bruckner was a late-bloomer. Many people do not know the name of Bruckner, but those who listen to classical music certainly know him. Bruckner lived in nineteenth-century Austria as a butcher and part-time organist. He was a very simple man. He always shaved his head and wore old clothes so as not to be mistaken for a person of wealth. Although his life was simple it was full. Yet, at the age of 41 he heard a performance of Richard Wagner's famous opera *Tristan and Isolde*. The experience transformed his life. He decided he would dedicate himself to musical composition. By the end of his life he had completed, among many other works, nine symphonies, three of which are still regularly played by orchestras around the world.

The world knows Albert Einstein as a genius in the field of science. This is certainly true, but he did not start out that way. As a boy growing up in Germany many people thought him to be ignorant. He failed courses in mathematics; he was very rebellious. As a boy he showed little evidence of the ability he possessed. Yet, it was Einstein's Theory of Relativity and similar ideas which brought about the nuclear age in which we now live.

Saint Augustine, one of the finest Christian minds and greatest saints who ever lived, was also a late-bloomer. Augustine wandered about for thirty years trying to find himself. He tried different religions, including paganism and the religion of the holy man Mani, known today as Manichaeism. He was involved in a relationship which produced a son. Eventually, through the prayers of his mother, Saint Monica, he was converted to Christianity. Saint Augustine's response to his conversion is a given in a famous line from his autobiography, *The Confessions*, "Late have I loved you, O Beauty ever ancient, ever new, late have I loved you!" Augustine became a bishop and a great scholar. He was one of the most famous men who ever lived.

Each of these men received an invitation. One invitation was to music, another was to science; the third was an invitation to greater service of God. These invitations were always present, because they were gifts from God. Once the gift was found it became a permanent part of who these people were.

In the Gospel, a parable familiar to most of us, we hear of God's invitation. The invitation may come at different times, early, late, or sometime in between. Whenever the invitation is received, however, the reward is the same.

2. There is a legend which says that when Saint Joseph, his wife the Blessed Virgin Mary, and Jesus were fleeing Israel to escape the clutches of King Herod, they stopped at a desert inn for food and water. Mary asked the lady of the inn for water in which to bathe her son. The lady provided the water and Mary bathed Jesus. The proprietor then asked if she might bathe her own son, suffering from leprosy, in the same waters used by Jesus. When she did the child was instantly made whole.

As time passed, the lady's son, named Dismas, matured into a strong man who became a thief and a murderer. He cared little for God or humans; he cared only for himself — his desires and needs.

He was a man devoid of compassion and many other positive virtues that most people possess. His life went in the opposite direction of Jesus, the one whom he had encountered without knowing it so many years before.

Many years later Dismas found himself in Jerusalem at the time of the Jewish Passover. Arrested for his crimes, he was convicted and sentenced to crucifixion, along with another criminal. Along the road to the mount called Calvary outside the city walls, another man joined the two convicted criminals, a certain Jesus of Nazareth who proclaimed that he was a king. Something told Dismas that this third man did not deserve to be there and to die in such an ignoble way. Something triggered his memory and he remembered his encounter with Jesus some 33 years ago. It was Jesus who had cured him; would he be willing to assist him again?

Saint Luke (23:39-43) tells us what happened: "One of the criminals who were hanged there kept deriding him and saying, 'Are you not the Messiah? Save yourself and us!' But the other rebuked him, saying, 'Do you not fear God, since you are under the same sentence of condemnation? And we indeed have been condemned justly, for we are getting what we deserve for our deeds, but this man has done nothing wrong.' Then he said, 'Jesus, remember me when you come into your kingdom.' Jesus replied, 'Truly I tell you, today you will be with me in Paradise.' "

A man whose life was by all standards a waste did not lose hope that Jesus might be able to save him. Such must be our attitude as well. Sometimes we feel that we have lost God's love and mercy, but such can never be the case, because God is all compassion and mercy. The parable of the laborers in the vineyard tells us that it is never too late to be with God!

Points Of Challenge And Questions To Ponder

1. All of us have received numerous invitations from the Lord to assist in God's work, to be present to others, to show the face of God to others. Have we accepted these invitations? Has our response been delayed? Have we rejected God's call outright?

2. Do we become jealous when we see people who enter the fold late? Do we ask ourselves why God would be merciful to such a person? Do we harbor anger as did Jonah against God for the mercy he demonstrated to the Ninevites?

3. Are we afraid to approach God because of past deeds that are inconsistent with the Christian message? Do we fear that Jesus can no longer love us because of the way we have rejected his call in the past?

4. Do we place limits on God? Do we not allow God to be infinite? Do we feel God must operate on the human level?

5. Do we believe that divine justice must triumph over compassion? Does the idea of equal pay or compensation for equal effort dominate our lives? Do we need to be converted to a broader understanding of God's infinite goodness in our world?

Exegesis And Explanation Of The Parable

The scene depicted in this parable reflects life in the Galilean countryside at the time of Jesus. The vineyard was probably a large piece of property where the owner employed a certain number of workers throughout the year. Now at the time of harvest, probably September, additional laborers are required to harvest the crop of grapes rapidly. Workers generally gathered in town centers at the outset of the day hoping that they could secure work. Thus, it would not have been uncommon for laborers to be found at all times of the day. In the time of Jesus, a day's labor was generally ten hours with the pay one denarius, a daily subsistence wage for the average family.

The familiar scene which Matthew describes in the parable cannot, however, mask several unusual and, for many, troublesome aspects of this pericope. First, this passage stands in sharp contrast to rabbinic parallels present in the literature of the day. The one most frequently referenced speaks of a laborer who is so efficient that the owner removes him from the others after only two hours of work and pays him a full day's wage on the grounds that he has done more in this short span than others will do in a full day. What Jesus teaches in this parable is exactly the opposite — God does not reward humans for efficiency, but rather out of overflowing grace. The equality of reward will be found in the Kingdom of Heaven. Listeners to this parable also noted that it was the landowner, not a servant, who went to the town to obtain workers.

Certainly the facet of the parable that was most troubling to those who lived in Jesus' day (and for us as well) is the apparent injustice that is done to those who have worked all day in the vineyard. The lesson of the parable is that grace supersedes impartial justice. The audience Jesus addressed was trained in the Jewish doctrine of merit, which maintained that people must accumulate to their credit numerous good deeds that could be converted into rewards before God. Matthew thus demonstrates the general doctrine that the rewards of God are not measured out according to number or the length of service. Rewards are subordinated to grace. The evangelist tells us that sacrifice and service will be honored by God, but the reward will far outdistance the work. Thus, God's action can only be seen as sheer grace. Although some may feel that their long and costly service qualifies them for a higher rate of pay (a greater reward in the Kingdom), we must acknowledge that all are eleventh-hour workers. None *deserve* the glorious future that God has prepared. God does not measure out a calculated portion of divine grace, but liberally grants gifts of forgiveness, reconciliation, peace, joy, and happiness.

The major difficulty for those who hear this parable is not the compassion demonstrated by God but the comparison made between those who came early and those who labored only a short time. The vineyard owner claims the right to pay his workers based on compassion, not on merit. Jesus certainly believed in justice, but divine compassion outshines divine justice. The point of the parable is that the owner deals not simply fairly but generously with the workers. Followers of Jesus must imitate such generosity, not begrudge it. Those who grumble base their contention on envy and a desire to weigh merit and reward neatly in adjusted scales. Free grace is measured against a bargaining spirit that expects something over and above the agreed upon wage for those who gained more merit by their longer service. The incomprehensible goodness of God itself becomes a stumbling block to those who refuse to relinquish human ideas of justice and merit. It does not matter how long and hard one has worked, only that one has been recruited and answered the call. Matthew does not tell us if those who grumble about their pay are later convinced of the owner's right to do as he does or to recognize the generosity extended to all. This question the evangelist leaves with his readers.

Matthew places this parable in a strategic location in his Gospel to illustrate some important points. The parable's location immediately after Matthew 19:16-30, where Jesus instructs outsiders and then answers Peter's question of what will be received by those who forfeit the world for the Lord, is doubtless intended to serve as a corrective to the concept of rewards. It also demonstrates that the priority the apostles possessed in their relationship with Jesus does not give them precedence of reward. The parable is clearly addressed to those who were critical of Jesus' work and opposed the proclamation of the Good News, generally thought to be the Pharisees. Matthew seeks to justify the gospel message and its favoring of Christians, the newcomers to the historical religious scene, against its critics. The parable may also have served as a defense by Jesus against his association with tax collectors and sinners. Possibly, as well, Matthew might be targeting Jewish Christians who were resentful of new leaders in the community who came from pagan backgrounds. These people, although they came late, would be acceptable in the Kingdom of Heaven. The divine favor of Christians is not unjust to the Jews, who have worked in God's vineyard longer, but did so to receive the agreed upon wage.

Allegory has been used in the past as a means to understand this parable. In the Patristic Church Irenaeus taught that the various hours when workers were hired represented historical periods of time from Adam forward, the eleventh hour being the period between the ascension and the Parousia.[1] Origen symbolized the time as different stages of human life at which people are called to Christianity. Others used allegory in time to trace how different people have been called to participate in and enjoy the divine plan.

The start of the day represents the divine contract which was Israel's charter with God. At this time laborers were hired on set terms, namely the Decalogue or Ten Commandments. As the historical day continues more are called, just as God called the prophets to do the Lord's work and proclaim the divine message. This happens three times at three-hour intervals. The last group, enlisted at the eleventh hour, a significant break in the orderly three-hour pattern, is the Christian community, which answered the call just before the end of time.

Today's biblical exegetes hold strong reservations on the use of allegory in this parable, save the idea that the parable speaks of the Kingdom of Heaven. The owner, representative of God, demonstrates that the justice of the world — namely greater merit for more work — is inconsistent with God's plan of the triumph of grace. In the Kingdom of Heaven the principles of merit and ability must be set aside so that grace can prevail. To measure God's goodness by human standards does not do justice to either side. People must never fail to understand that God gives infinitely more than a just wage. God's goodness exceeds all human conception of graciousness. True Christians cannot find fault with God's grace or its measure to those who come at a late hour. The addition of converts to the church must be a source of joy; it must not be a matter of skepticism.

Context Of The Parable

Context In The Church Year

This pericope is presented as the second of five consecutive Sunday readings that highlight the parables of Matthew. This passage is framed by two parables which bring it context, the unlimited forgiveness of God and the need to cast off self-righteousness. The parable of the laborers in the vineyard demonstrates, like the parable of unlimited forgiveness, that humans must not limit God. God's ways and actions are far beyond our conception, but this does not mean that we can limit God to what we can perceive, see, feel, hear, or experience in any way. Additionally, this parable serves as a good prelude to the parable to be presented next week, a warning against self-righteousness. Heritage and the past favor of God do not guarantee entry into the Kingdom of Heaven. What is necessary is a conversion of heart, not reliance upon past glory or greatness.

Context With Other Gospels

The parable of the laborers in the vineyard is unique to Matthew, but some of the ideas in the passage are found in other Gospels and canonical books of the Bible. Mark 10:31 speaks of the first being last and the last being first, an idea which Matthew intentionally reverses to make his point that coming late to the fold will in no way ill affect the reward that is rendered. This parable can also be paralleled in part to Luke's story of the Prodigal Son, where the grumbling of the day workers can be compared with the complaint of the elder son against his brother and his father (15:29). The warning against those who grumble is found in similar terms in Luke 5:30, John 6:41ff, and 1 Corinthians 10:10. The whole parable is in some ways an exposition of Ecclesiastes 5:12: "Sweet is the sleep of laborers, whether they eat little or much; but the surfeit of the rich will not let them sleep."

An implicit issue in this parable is the ancient understanding of bargaining with God. In ancient Rome humans bargained with the gods to obtain what they wanted. Sacrifice would be rendered with a certain expectation of return. This same idea is found in the Old Testament. In Genesis 28:18-22, for example, Jacob attempts to bargain with God. He asks for protection and sustenance, promising to reward God with a tithe of his income. Job also addresses this issue (1:9) with his words, "Does Job fear God for nothing?"

Context With First And Second Lessons

First Lesson: Jonah 3:10—4:11. This passage from Jonah serves as an excellent support to the parable of the laborers in the vineyard. Jonah was successful in his assigned mission to preach repentance and conversion to the people of Nineveh, but with his task completed the prophet is upset that God is merciful. Like those hired first in the parable, Jonah is upset at the compassion God shows to those who come late into the fold. He goes off to be alone and brood, but God pursues him. The prophet must be taught a lesson by God concerning the triumph of compassion over perceived justice. Rather than rejoicing at what God did through his actions, Jonah selfishly believes God is not fair. Jonah bases his understanding on human justice, a finite and prejudicial justice. In the end God teaches Jonah, as Jesus through Matthew teaches us, that God does no injustice in demonstrating mercy, compassion, forgiveness, and kindness.

Second Lesson: Philippians 1:21-30. The Apostle to the Gentiles provides much food for thought in this powerful passage. Paul tells the Christian community at Philippi that he must persevere to bring joy and progress to the faith, even though he has a desire to be freed from this life and be with Christ. He then exhorts the people to conduct themselves in ways consistent with the gospel of Christ. They are not to be intimidated by opponents, for it is a special privilege to take Christ's part in suffering through a consistent promotion of the gospel message.

Paul's message relates well to the challenge presented in the parable of the laborers in the vineyard. The people are to act as Christ in welcoming those who come late to the banquet of life. Jesus did not begrudge any converts, but rather treated all with respect, whether they came at the beginning or the eleventh hour. The reward is the same for all; God does no injustice to anyone in demonstrating compassion. The care and divine justice of God must be the goal we set for our actions.

---

1. The first four periods as outlined by Irenaeus were: Dawn — the time of Adam; hours 9 to 12 — the period of Noah to Abraham; hours 12 to 3 — the period of Abraham to Moses; hours 3 to 5 — the period of Moses to Christ.

Chapter 9

Actions Speak Louder Than Words

Matthew 21:28-32

"What do you think? A man had two sons; he went to the first and said, 'Son, go and work in the vineyard today.' He answered, 'I will not'; but later he changed his mind and went. The father went to the second and said the same; and he answered, 'I go, sir'; but he did not go. Which of the two did the will of his father?" They said, "The first." Jesus said to them, "Truly I tell you, the tax collectors and the prostitutes are going into the kingdom of God ahead of you. For John came to you in the way of righteousness and you did not believe him, but the tax collectors and the prostitutes believed him; and even after you saw it, you did not change your minds and believe him."

Theme

We have all heard the adage that actions speak louder than words. Today we are presented in the daily newspaper headlines with numerous incidents where the actions of people are inconsistent with the words they profess. We are also bombarded with the idea that reward must follow any action. Society tells us that tasks are not worth our effort unless there is a pot of gold or some other significant prize that awaits the completion of our effort. We who bear the name Christian must stand against this tide of rhetoric and reward and profess by action as well as word our faith in Jesus.

Christians must be willing to do what is right because it is right. The reward in this life may at times be the cross of ridicule or rejection, but we can expect no better lot than the one we follow. Conversion to a life of action consistent with the ideas we express on our lips will one day bring us to God and eternal life.

Spiritual Food For The Journey

Martin Luther King, Jr., leader of the American civil rights movement from December 1955 until his assassination in April 1968, often echoed the conviction of Mahatma Gandhi, the great Indian freedom fighter, one generation earlier: "We have the right to protest for right." The civil rights movement in the United States demonstrated how a people long denied freedom and the inalienable rights guaranteed by the Declaration of Independence — life, liberty, and the pursuit of happiness — were able to use nonviolent protest to change unjust laws and practices and transform the minds of many to a more equitable understanding of life. Dr. King firmly believed that his philosophy of nonviolence, derived from many sources in his educational development, would be effective if actions were consistent with words. When he electrified a crowd of some 200,000 people in August 1963 with his famous "I Have a Dream" speech during the March on Washington, King laid the groundwork for future years that would ultimately bring the end to "Jim Crow" and at least a beginning to the conversion of America's penchant toward racism.

We all know that actions do speak loudly, but most would have to admit a certain reticence in action. Action exposes to the whole world what we truly believe. It is rather easy and unthreatening to make comments and address issues in the forum of debate, but the transfer of words to personal involvement is often complex and we hesitate in action. While words can be cheap, action is quite costly. It costs us time and effort; it may even cost us friends. Doing what is right simply because it is right must be the attitude we possess. As important as conviction is, such deep-seated belief holds little value unless we can support our words with effort and devotion to cause.

The philosophy of Martin Luther King, Jr., transformed a nation; the combination of words and action on our part can aid the conversion of society to a more God-centered understanding of the world. If we speak but demonstrate no complementary action, those who hear us will wonder at our own level of commitment and may question our conviction. If, however, we can demonstrate by what we do that we choose and act rightly simply because it is right and with no thought to personal gain, then our world will become a better place and the Kingdom of God on earth will be one step closer to reality.

Application Of The Parable To Contemporary Life

Sermon Openings
1. In a vast field that stretched as far as the eye could see, a great multitude of people milled about waiting for something to happen. Quite unexpectedly a messenger came into the midst of the people and announced, "You are to walk around this field 25 times carrying a baton." The people were a bit mystified by these words and asked, "What will happen when we finish?" "You will learn the answer when you are done," came the reply. So the crowd ambled off to make its first lap of the field. As they walked they passed the baton amongst themselves. It took almost a full day at a leisurely pace to walk around the field, but they eventually made the circuit of the field the first time. This feat called for a celebration.

As the crowd celebrated they decided, just for the heck of it, to make the next lap more interesting. They broke into teams to race against each other. The task would not be so boring and winners and losers could be determined. This would transform a mundane task into a fun-filled event. So the people separated themselves into five teams, the Reds, Yellows, Blacks, Browns, and Whites. There were some in the great multitude, however, who refused to join the teams. They called themselves "The Others" because they did something different than the teams. Strangely, it was The Others who were given the baton to carry, since the teams argued amongst themselves over which team should have it. The five teams, the Reds, Yellows, Blacks, Browns, and Whites, took their marks and then took off at breakneck speed. The Yellow team won the second lap. The teams decided after that second circuit of the field, just for the heck of it, that they would station various members of each team at select sites around the field. In this way no one would have to run the whole distance but rather each would run an individual segment of the whole. Thus, the relay race was invented. As the five teams raced around the field in relays, The Others simply continued on their way around the field. The teams thought The Others were "out of it."

The competition among the teams became more and more intense. Soon the racing teams realized that slow runners were a liability to the team's chances to win. They decided, therefore, that only the fast runners would compete. This, however, did not seem to satisfy those who were the best on each team, so it was decided, just for the heck of it, that each team would be represented by one individual and races would be held in measured distances. On one lap the representative of the Browns won and on another it was the Yellow team member who was victorious. Meanwhile, The Others continued to plod their way around the field, lap after lap after lap. When they completed all 25 laps they threw a party. When the messenger arrived in the midst of the celebration The Others asked, "You told us at the beginning that we would learn our reward when we finished. We have completed the 25 laps of the field. What will we get?" "Your reward," said the messenger, "is that you made it." The Others were stunned. "Is that all there is? We have made this long journey just to say we made it?" When The Others thought about their accomplishment, however, they had to agree that this was the reason they were celebrating — because they had made it. "But what about the teams?" asked one of The Others, seeing that none of them were present. "The teams," said the messenger, "as you can see, didn't make it. And that's the heck of it!"[1]

Completing a task, making no attempt to gain personal glory, doing what is right simply because it is the right thing to do — these are some of the important ideas brought to light by John Aurelio's thought-provoking story, "The Game." Today's parable of the two sons presents a similar message.

114

2. "Free at last, free at last — thank God Almighty we are free at last." With these words Martin Luther King, Jr., ended his most famous speech. Given at the foot of the Lincoln Memorial on the Washington Mall in August 1963, it was the last event of the "March on Washington," the highpoint of the American civil rights movement. Martin Luther King, Jr., was its principal symbol and spokesman. Dr. King called the nation to reform, but he did it in a way which was new to American history. He advocated non-violence and civil disobedience, in line with some of the great thinkers of the past whom he had studied, including the great Indian freedom fighter Mahatma Gandhi and the American philosopher Henry David Thoreau. Dr. King said that the nation's system of racial segregation, which had been labeled the "Jim Crow" laws, had to cease. It could no longer be business as usual. As Abraham Lincoln a century earlier had told the nation it could not live half slave and half free, so Martin Luther King, Jr. said the nation could no longer live separate and unequal; racial segregation had to end.

Dr. King's campaign for civil rights began quite unexpectedly in December 1955 when Rosa Parks said she would not move to the back of a Montgomery city bus. The drive went to Greensboro, North Carolina, and Albany, Georgia. There was the "Freedom Ride" of 1961, the marches in Birmingham and Washington, and the voter registration drive in Mississippi and the protest march from Selma to Montgomery, Alabama. The campaign eventually arrived in Memphis, Tennessee, in April 1968 when Dr. King came to support a sanitation workers' strike. There he was assassinated at the tender age of 39. The night before he died, however, Dr. King gave another of his electrifying speeches, where he said, "I have been to the mountaintop and I've seen the other side." Martin Luther King, Jr., believed his cause to be right, that a new day was necessary in America, and that a highway of justice needed to be constructed for all people.

Martin Luther King, Jr., professed in word and action what he believed. He courageously challenged a reluctant nation to transform itself, to be converted to a belief in equality for all people, not only those who by tradition had been the culturally elite. Dr. King told America that it had the right to protest for right. In today's parable of the two sons, Jesus suggests that our actions must be consistent with our words, that we must do what is right because it is right.

Points Of Challenge And Questions To Ponder

1. Are we long on words but short on action? Do we feel comfortable giving our opinion or providing advice but refuse to back up our words with effort?

2. Are our actions consistent with our words or do we exhibit a Jekyll and Hyde division in our lives? Are people attracted to what we do or can they see through the exterior veneer that we present?

3. Are status, reward, name, and achievement important to us? Can we live our daily lives and desire no recompense for our efforts? Can we see the need to do what is right simply because it is the right thing to do?

4. If we observe inconsistency in what people say and do, are we willing to challenge the individual or do we let it slide? Can we take the initiative to call people to task for what they do?

5. Are we more concerned with what people think of us or the accomplishment of our tasks? Can we place attitudes towards others and desire for personal accomplishment to one side in order to complete the tasks life throws our way? Are we more interested in looks and appearance as compared with getting the job done?

Exegesis And Explanation Of The Parable

The parable of the two sons, exclusive to Matthew's Gospel, is the first of three parables addressed to the chief priests and elders of Israel that form a response to their challenge to Jesus' authority. The Jewish leaders want to know by what authority Jesus acts and speaks. In this pericope we see how Jesus demonstrates the failure of Israel in the past to recognize the authority of John the Baptist and others who have come in God's name. Their words have been significant and proper, but their actions have been inconsistent with what they preach. The parable is marked by simplicity and can be summarized in the familiar words of Saint James (1:22-25):

> *But be doers of the word, and not merely hearers who deceive themselves. For if any are hearers of the word and not doers, they are like those who look at themselves in a mirror; for they look at themselves and, on going away, immediately forget what they were like. But those who look into the perfect law, the law of liberty, and persevere, being not hearers who forget but doers who act — they will be blessed in their doing.*

The parable teaches that the person who refuses to do what is asked, but subsequently changes one's mind and does the task, is better than the one who promises to carry out obligations but never fulfills them. The contrast between verbal rebellion and ultimate obedience as opposed to verbal obedience and failure to act is clear. In other words, the parable of the two sons illustrates one aspect of the traditional adage, "Practice what you preach."

The parable of the two sons as it is presented in most contemporary translations of the Bible is different than many ancient manuscripts. *The New English Bible*, for example, follows Patristic texts which reverse the order of the two sons, with the second being the one who initially refused to go but eventually went to the vineyard to work. This alternative form reflects an allegorical interpretation of the parable from the ancient church. The Jews claimed to be obedient to God, but rejected the gospel. The Gentiles, coming on the scene later, refused to obey God, but repented and accepted the gospel. *The Revised Standard Version* of the pericope is preferred because in its ordering of the two sons the story is less contrived since the father only seeks help from the second son when the first refuses to go when he is asked.

Scholars disagree on the ultimate source of this parable. Some suggest that the passage has its roots in Jesus' own words, but the preponderance of opinion suggests that Matthew created the parable to illustrate his basic theme that God requires deeds rather

117

than empty words. Use of the term "Kingdom of God" in this passage differs from the normal "Kingdom of Heaven" and suggests Matthew's hand in composition. The vocabulary and style of this passage are similar to other sections of the Gospel which have been attributed to Matthew's original hand. The parable presupposes the rejection of Jesus' authority on the part of Israel. This would only have been known by a writer like Matthew composing his Gospel after the death, resurrection, and ascension of Jesus. Certain difficulties in the parable also illustrate its probable origin with the evangelist. It is hardly likely that the chief priests and elders *en masse* were guilty of failing in their duties to God; most carried out the public duties appointed to them. Additionally, there is nothing to indicate that John the Baptist or Jesus managed to effect a mass conversion of tax collectors and prostitutes. Scholars believe Matthew used generic images to demonstrate his understanding of Jesus' message.

Certain biblical exegetes today suggest that the parable was presented by Matthew to distinguish Jesus' teaching from a contemporary Jewish story. In the latter, humility is the virtue that is stressed. Five people are asked to complete a task. The first four refuse because they are uncertain they can complete the assignment; the fifth accepts the task but does not perform it, laying himself open to the wrath of the king who assigned the work. Jesus' version of the story, as told by Matthew, brings infinitely more comfort in its demonstration that there truly are obedient disciples among those who would never claim to be. Jesus thus invites into his family and life those considered by the religious authorities of his day to be outsiders.

The parable proper (verses 28 to 31) uses the figure of two sons to represent two kinds of people. The religious leaders of the day who made formal professions of piety but failed to do what God required are contrasted with tax collectors and prostitutes who did not follow the law, but repented in response to preaching and were now keeping the commandments. The first son is the personification of tax collectors and prostitutes who are living sinful lives and have refused to do God's will. However, when John the Baptist came "proclaiming a baptism of repentance for the forgiveness of sins" (Mark 1:4), these social and moral outcasts of society repented, believed, and thus by their actions gained access to the Kingdom of God. They did the will of the Father. The second son portrays the attitude of the religious leaders of Jesus' day. They do everything for others to see: "They do all their deeds to be seen by others; for they make their phylacteries broad and their fringes long. They love to have the place of honor at banquets and the best seats in the synagogues, and to be greeted with respect in the marketplaces, and to have people call them rabbi" (Matthew 23:5-7). They do not practice what they preach. John came to show them the way of righteousness; they listened but refused to believe.

Jesus attacks those who believed themselves to be fulfilling the will of God but were not and commends those who felt excluded from Israel but were actually fulfilling the will of God. The parable presents harsh judgment upon those who say "yes" verbally and intellectually without seeing that the will of God is realized in their lives. In the parable this is demonstrated by the contrast between outward conformity on the one hand and actual work on the other. In other words, formal, legal, and ritual observance of God's requirements is contrasted with repentance which leads to true service of God and God's people. At the same time this passage is an urgent call to place into action what God directs in the Scripture. The parable thus contrasts the "devout" who rejected Jesus with those considered sinners who accepted him. Thus, tax collectors and prostitutes enter the Kingdom of God before the so-called "righteous." This is the miracle at which angels (Luke 15:7, 10) and God the Father (Luke 15:23-24) rejoice in heaven. In this way Jesus defines the requirement for entry into eternal life as doing the will of the Father. Access to God is not gained by professions of obedience that are not matched by actions.

Jesus, the great teacher, uses this parable to help people teach themselves about the real meaning and extent of their own religious ideas and to answer his questions. In asking "Which of the two did the will of his Father?" (21:31) the chief priests and elders of the Jews can no longer hide behind feigned ignorance. The Lord forces them to answer, even though they realize the parable describes them and their failures. Jesus wishes to teach Israel about its failure and to show the nation that it needs the instruction and example of Jesus. The Lord attacks not the refusal to obey God but the religious hierarchy's rejection of God's call to conversion.

Context Of The Parable

Context In The Church Year

The church places this parable in the third week of five consecutive Sundays that feature parables in Matthew's Gospel. The parable of the two sons, although in the center of the group, serves as the first of three pericopes specially designed to illustrate the authority of Jesus in his ministry. Challenged by the religious authorities of his day, Christ responds with an indictment of those very officials and exposes their failure to demonstrate properly by action the words they profess. In the last two Sundays we have heard about God's unlimited forgiveness and the triumph of compassion over justice. The church has shown the munificence and greatness of God's love for us; now it is time for us to respond and manifest by our actions what our words profess. As God first loved us, so we are now asked to love God and God's people, not only by what we say, but more especially by what we do.

Context With Other Gospels

Matthew drew from his private source to write the parable of the two sons. Although no other evangelist presents this pericope, commentators have discovered parallels to the basic themes of acting on God's word and conversion in both the Old and New Testaments. In the Hebrew Scriptures we learn of the need to obey the Word of God, heed the Lord's voice, and do God's will. Samuel tells Saul, "Has the Lord as great delight in burnt offerings and sacrifices, as in obeying the voice of the Lord? Surely, to obey is better than sacrifice, and to heed than the fat of rams" (1 Samuel 15:22). Scripture scholars also see a parallel between the parable of the two sons and the story of Nathan and David in 2 Samuel chapter 12. In John's Gospel (15:14) Jesus instructs his disciples, "You are my friends if you do what I command you." Similarity is also present between this parable and the more famous story of the Prodigal Son in Luke 15:11-32. Mark 12:1-12 presents the familiar theme of the Jews' rejection of God's prophets and their final rejection of God's son, resulting in Israel's replacement by others, namely the Gentiles.

Context With First And Second Lessons
First Lesson: Ezekiel 18:1-4, 25-32. Ezekiel's prophecy in chapter 18 describes a message quite similar to that illustrated by the parable of the two sons. The prophet speaks of conversion and the ultimate actions of people in turning to God. Transformation of one's life away from iniquity to righteousness is what Ezekiel suggests will preserve life. One may speak the right words, but if there is no conversion in the heart, then the hollowness of one's life is revealed. The prophet tells the people to repent, cast away all transgressions, and seek a new heart and spirit.

Ezekiel's words challenge us to complete the tasks of life simply because they are asked of us. What is important is to do the right thing, regardless of how others perceive us — as saint or sinner. Actions are more important than any labels people may give us. To live in the sight of God requires that we carry out the precepts of the Lord.

Second Lesson: Philippians 2:1-13. The famous Christological hymn of Saint Paul in his Letter to the Philippians clearly demonstrates Jesus' understanding that actions speak louder than words. Jesus, the Son of God, came to us as a man; he emptied himself of divinity to take on the human condition. The Lord died an ignominious death on the cross to save us from our sins. Jesus did not have to save the world in this fashion; he chose to suffer and die. His actions were consistent with his words; he practiced what he preached. Jesus did what was right simply because it was right. He sought no glory and received none in this life, but his salvific death through obedience to the will of the Father made salvation possible for us. May we rejoice and be glad because of what God has done for us.

---

1. Paraphrased from "The Game," in John R. Aurelio, *Colors! Stories of the Kingdom* (New York: The Crossroad Publishing Company, 1993), pp. 81-84.

Chapter 10

Caring For The Gifts Of God

Matthew 21:33-43

"Listen to another parable. There was a landowner who planted a vineyard, put a fence around it, dug a wine press in it, and built a watchtower. Then he leased it to tenants and went to another country. When the harvest time had come, he sent his slaves to the tenants to collect his produce. But the tenants seized his slaves and beat one, killed another, and stoned another. Again he sent other slaves, more than the first; and they treated them in the same way. Finally he sent his son to them, saying, 'They will respect my son.' But when the tenants saw the son, they said to themselves, 'This is the heir; come, let us kill him and get his inheritance.' So they seized him, threw him out of the vineyard, and killed him. Now when the owner of the vineyard comes, what will he do to those tenants?" They said to him, "He will put those wretches to a miserable death, and lease the vineyard to other tenants who will give him the produce at harvest time."

Jesus said to them, "Have you never read in the Scriptures: 'The stone that the builders rejected has become the cornerstone; this was the Lord's doing, and it is amazing in our eyes'? Therefore I tell you, the kingdom of God will be taken away from you and given to a people that produces the fruits of the kingdom."

123

Theme

God has provided us with all that is necessary for life. Some receive many gifts and talents and others receive few, but all receive what we need. In our hedonistic and highly self-motivated society we tend to forget that gifts are provided for the benefit of all and not a select few. Using God's gifts wisely, fully, and for the betterment of our world is a constant challenge and one that necessitates constant vigilance and reflection.

Spiritual Food For The Journey

The United States has always been known, especially to immigrants, as the land of opportunity. Throughout our nation's history, people, operating under the banner of the "Protestant work ethic," have labored long and hard to provide for immediate family needs and to build futures in a land where all is possible for those who are willing to work. Many "Horatio Alger" stories, describing the heroic efforts of people, exist. They inspire us to do our best and produce much.

There is no question that America is a land of plenty that has produced an abundance for many for almost 225 years. Personal effort and achievement in our land, as well intentioned as it generally is, can lead, if we are not careful, to a selfish attitude toward what we have. We can become possessive of opportunity, position, relationships, and certainly material things. All we have, however, comes from God and thus is given for the benefit of all God's people. Attitudes which say "I worked hard and I deserve it" are inconsistent with Jesus' message that sharing all that we have helps build the road that leads to eternal life. God has provided us with gifts to the extent that we can use them, not for personal gain alone, but to build the Kingdom of God in our world.

The parable of the wicked tenants demonstrates how God was displeased with the people of Israel because of their selfish use of the gifts provided to them. We must learn a lesson from Scripture that God asks us to use opportunities and gifts properly and wisely. What we have is given by God; let us make our best effort to return the fruit of our labor to God and all God's people.

Application Of The Parable To Contemporary Life

Sermon Openings
1. "Use it or lose it." We have all heard this expression, said it ourselves, and applied it more than once. The words tell us that it is necessary rightly and fully to use the gifts given us by God. We are challenged to use God's gifts for the betterment of all and for our own growth in the Spirit. If we fail to use properly and fully or abuse the gifts of God they will be taken away.

There are many examples of how the gifts of God have been left dormant or abused with adverse results for all. In Greek mythology we remember the story of Icarus and Daedelus. This father and son were given the ability to fly by the gods. It was a special gift that set them apart from all other humans. But they abused the gift, thinking that with their special ability they could be like the gods and fly to the sun. As they rose high in the sky their wings began to melt; the great gift was lost.

Position in society and the power and authority that come with it are often abused. Throughout history there have been many examples of leaders who have been invested with power and authority, have used it to abuse people, and who in the end lost the gift entrusted to them. Many of the kings in Israel rejected the warnings of the prophets, abused the people, and turned away from God. Their fate was death, punishment of future generations, and ultimately exile of the Hebrew people to Babylon. In our own twentieth century we recall all too well the terror inflicted upon the world by dictators such as Adolf Hitler and Benito Mussolini. Their abuse of power led to their ultimate demise. In our own country the Watergate scandal demonstrated the abuse of executive privilege. The shock of a nation that its leader might be a criminal was magnified when Richard Nixon resigned, the only President to leave office as a result of alleged wrongdoing.

In our own lives we can think of examples of how we have failed to use properly or fully or possibly have abused God's gifts. Most of us have studied languages, but few of us today can use what we learned in high school or college Spanish, French, or German class. The gift of reading or speaking another tongue must be exercised or it will be lost. If we have the ability to shoot a sub-par round on the golf course, but refuse to practice this skill, then the next time we "hit the links" the results will not be what we want or expect. As the expression goes, use it or lose it.

Today's readings challenge us to use the gifts of God wisely or they will be taken away.

2. Is the life you lead now the life for which you want to be remembered? That very challenging and thought-provoking question certainly came to the mind of the famous Swedish scientist Alfred Nobel one day. In the common everyday exercise of reading the morning paper Nobel discovered the challenge of God before his very eyes.

Nobel was born in 1833 to a scientist and his wife. From his earliest days it was evident to everyone that Alfred was a gifted young man. He read voraciously all the books and periodicals he could find; he excelled in literature. By the time he was fifteen years old he could read, write, and speak four languages besides his native Swedish. Although he showed promise in the humanities area, it was his love of science and his desire to be an inventor, like his father, that most excited him.

When Nobel was sixteen he had exhausted the educational possibilities of his native district in Sweden. He decided to move away for more training. He first went to Paris and then across the Atlantic to the United States, where he spent four years studying science and engineering principles, ideas that had become that much more important after the onset of the Industrial Revolution in the late eighteenth and early nineteenth centuries.

With his education complete, Nobel returned to his native land. He began to tinker around in his laboratory, creating an invention or two, but nothing of any significance. In the 1860s, however, he began to conduct experiments with nitroglycerin, a highly volatile and unstable substance. One experiment produced an explosion and Alfred's younger brother was killed. The experience crushed Nobel in one way, but in another it was the catalyst to find a way to harness the energy of this substance and make it of practical use to the world.

Nobel discovered a functional use of nitroglycerin, but it came about quite accidentally. One day in his workshop, he noticed that some of the nitroglycerin, which is a liquid at room temperature, had leached into some packing material which surrounded the many bottles of chemicals sent him for his various experiments. Nobel found that this third substance, made from the initial two, had all the energy capacity and blasting potential of nitroglycerin, but it was stable and thus could be better controlled. Without knowing it, Alfred Nobel had invited dynamite.

The uses of dynamite throughout the world made Nobel a rich and famous man overnight. Mountains could be blasted away to make room for railroads. Of equal use, however, was the placement of dynamite in bombs, projectiles, and other weapons of war. With patents received in 1867 and 1868, first in the United States and later in Great Britain, for dynamite and blasting caps, Nobel gained great notoriety. With the discovery of oil on land he owned in the state of Russia, Nobel became one of the richest men in the world. He could sit back, relax, and enjoy life.

Alfred's serenity came to an abrupt halt one day when he picked up the morning paper. The headline read, "Dynamite King Dies." The story and obituary in the paper were erroneous; he was alive and well. Nobel decided to read the article, however, in order to know what people would think of him after his death. Besides all the normal facts and dates of an obituary, Nobel read a description which labeled him as the "merchant of death." The expression disturbed the scientist greatly. Certainly the comment came in reference to his association with dynamite, but this did not lighten the blow. Nobel realized at that moment that the life he had led was not the life for which he wanted to be remembered.

Something needed to be done to correct this attitude. The past was history; its record was etched in stone. The future was something, however, over which Nobel had some control. Alfred was a rich man. How could his money be put to a positive use? He decided to change his will. He left his vast fortune in trust to a committee which each year would select people who, in theory and practice, had made positive contributions to the furthering of humankind. Thus, in 1901, five years after his death, the first Nobel

127

Prizes were awarded, initially in five areas: physics, chemistry, literature, medicine, and the famous Nobel Peace Prize. Later, in 1968 and thereafter, a prize in economics was added.

Alfred Nobel had experienced conversion. God had been challenging him in many ways, but he never took the time, nor realized the significance of God's presence. He was determined not to allow the presence of God to pass him by again!

Is the life you lead the life for which you want to be remembered? The same question that haunted Alfred Nobel must be our question as well. Alfred Nobel was given many great gifts but needed conversion in order to use them wisely. What will it take for us?

Points Of Challenge And Questions To Ponder

1. Are we selfish with the gifts provided us by God? Do we use these gifts for ourselves alone or do we make every effort to share our time, talents, and resources with others?

2. Are we lazy and through neglect do we fail to use God's gifts? Have we been remiss in our duty to provide for others?

3. Are we willing to serve others when called upon by the local community and/or the church? Do we opt out, saying we are too busy, when the true reason is we don't want to get involved?

4. Do we take care of ourselves so that we can effectively use God's gifts? Do we hurt ourselves through lack of sleep or exercise or overuse of alcohol, tobacco, or other chemicals?

5. Do we give God sufficient time in our lives? Do we make a concerted effort to build the Kingdom on earth? Do we slight God in favor of personal gain or pleasure?

Exegesis And Explanation Of The Parable

The parable of the wicked tenants is the centerpiece of Jesus' threefold response to the chief priests and elders who challenge his authority. Like the parables of the two sons and the king's wedding feast which precede and follow this passage, this pericope is a parable of judgment. Scholars disagree on the application of Jesus' words of judgment because of the uncertain allegorical nature of the parable. Clearly, however, the passage is Matthew's attempt to demonstrate Jesus' dissatisfaction with the Jews' response to his teaching.

The parable offers a true picture of rural life in Galilee in apostolic times, but not without some inconsistencies. There were lands, held by absentee landowners, which were worked by peasants on a system similar to sharecropping. Rent was paid by workers through a fixed amount of produce or as a percentage of the entire crop. It is not unlikely that at times there were violent assaults upon agents who came to collect the rent. Matthew thus used images and situations that allowed his readers, generally thought to be Aramaic-speaking converts to Christianity, to understand better Jesus' words of admonition and warning. At this point allegory appears to be the purpose of the evangelist. It is unlikely that the response of the owner to violence would have been to send more agents, and then later, when problems were not resolved, his son. Still, some exegetes have viewed the parable as a realistic description of the revolutionary attitude of Galilean peasants toward foreign landlords.

Scholars agree that the parable is allegorical, but opinions differ on the intent of Matthew in this passage. The significance of the vineyard is uncertain, but the echo of Isaiah's Song of the Vineyard (5:1-7), where the vineyard represents Israel, is recognizable. Unlike Isaiah, however, the vineyard in Matthew's parable has produced the expected fruit; the problem lies with the refusal of the peasants to remit the owner's share of the produce to the agents. The tenant farmers have generally been understood to represent Israel's religious leaders who, despite their alleged loyalty to the Torah, fail to give God his due by believing in God's present activity in the world, manifest in the ministries of John the Baptist and Jesus. Although the chief priests and elders have been charged with the responsibility of leading Israel in the way of righteousness, they have in fact rebelled against God and will be replaced. The chief feature of the allegory is the violent treatment of the owner's slaves, including the son. Most biblical experts agree that reference is made here to Israel's persecution of the prophets sent to it by God (1 Kings 19:10, 14; 2 Chronicles 24:18-22, 36:15-16; Acts 7:51-53).

The principal area of disagreement in the allegorical interpretation of this parable is the question of who will lose the kingdom. In verse 43 we read how the Kingdom of God will be taken "from you [collectively] and given to a people that produces the fruits of the kingdom." Although Jesus specifically addresses "the chief priests and elders" (v. 23), the tradition of the prophets (especially as understood in verse 43) suggests that behind the leaders stands the whole generation of rebellious Israel. Many scholars thus suggest that the evangelist is making an indictment of the whole nation, not merely its leaders. Thus, Israel will be replaced by the Gentile church. Other exegetes state that it is incorrect to assume the transfer is to the Gentiles alone. For Matthew the church is not Jew or Gentile; it is a new community that transcends segregation and traditional groupings of peoples. Despite the differences of opinion it is clear that Matthew believes the Kingdom will be taken from those who reject Jesus and given to a people who have listened to Christ's message and can bear much fruit.

The use of Psalm 118 (verse 42), a passage well-known to the Jews of Jesus' day, gives additional evidence to the belief that the Kingdom will be transferred to a new people. Jesus' rhetorical question had to be answered in the affirmative. The imagery is shifted from the tenants who rejected the servants to the builders who rejected the stone. The tenants, by killing the son, destroyed themselves, while the builders who rejected the stone which became the capstone made themselves appear to be foolish. Exegetes generally agree that as the verse reads it can only refer to the admission of the Gentile church. However, scholars point out that this verse and verse 43 are probably later expansions of the original parable added to demonstrate Jesus' favor of the Gentiles.

The possible extrapolation of the parable to the early church situation raises the question of what the original parable intended. Some biblical exegetes state that the original parable of Jesus can be discovered in the repeated call for due return on the use of gifts provided God in the vineyard. In each successive case the deliberate refusal of the tenants is met with increased violence. When refusal to cooperate does not result in punishment, but only further requests, the tenants begin to feel secure. They forget that they are tenants and make plans to use the vineyard, which they do not own, as their own property. Jesus' message gains strength since the wickedness of the tenants consists not only in keeping for themselves any produce, but also in claiming the whole enterprise as their own. The Lord's message of misuse of God-given gifts is highlighted in this parable.

If a message warning the Jews of their misuse of God's gifts was Jesus' original intent in the parable, then, as many scholars have suggested, the sending of the son is a secondary feature of the pericope. It reflects the interpretation of the death of Christ in relation to Israel's whole history. The parable thus does not look forward to the death of Jesus, but looks back to it and sees it (from the perspective of the apostolic church in its continuing conflict with Judaism) as the climactic event in a long history of the rejection of God's prophets. It was bad enough to kill the prophets, but infinitely worse to murder the son. This is clearly a creation of the early church and Matthew's attempt to demonstrate Jewish complicity in the death of Christ. In the past this understanding has fueled the fires of anti-Semitism, leading in more recent years to a changed interpretation for the sending of the son. Scholars suggest that although there is no reason for anti-Semitism, it is wrong to change what Matthew apparently meant, if indeed he believed that God had rejected Israel and replaced it with the church (Jew and Gentile) because of the death of Jesus.

Scripture exegetes provide additional evidence that the death of the son is a creation of the Apostolic Church and not a prediction of Jesus. The allegory that suggests that the tenants would inherit the vineyard at the death of the son does not make sense. Nothing in Hebrew law of the day would have designated tenants as the heirs to the vineyard. Thus, it appears that the passage about the son was added later by Matthew to highlight his message of the ill will of the tenants who represented Israel.

131

Context Of The Parable

Context In The Church Year

As the centerpiece of a trilogy of parables on judgment, the story of the wicked tenants is chosen by the church to continue to challenge our sensibilities and to encourage personal and communal growth in the Lord. Jesus tells this parable and those that frame it on both sides to demonstrate his authority. Last week we heard of harsh judgment for those whose actions and words are inconsistent. Today we are told that God's gifts must not be taken for granted. Next week we will realize our need to be ready for God's call, for many are called but few are chosen.

The Christian community needs to be reminded of our place in God's plan. As God's greatest creation our place is integral and extremely important, but we cannot lose sight of the fact that we are creatures and thus subject to God's law and judgment. In its wisdom the church presents this series of parables from Matthew's Gospel to encourage us to renew our attitudes and review our actions to assure that we are on the correct road. We must remind ourselves that our mission is to build God's kingdom, not our own.

Context With Other Gospels

The parable of the wicked tenants is provided in four versions: the Synoptic writers and the apocryphal Gospel of Thomas. Mark 12:1-12, Luke 20:9-19, and the Gospel of Thomas (Saying 65) present this parable with slight differences that provide various interpretations. In Luke and Thomas there is no reference to Isaiah's "Song of the Vineyard." Another difference between Matthew and Luke compared with Mark is found in the murder of the son. Mark places the crime in the vineyard, while the other Synoptics say the son was dragged outside the vineyard and killed. The latter version is clearly an illustration of the apostolic church allegorizing the son to Jesus who was crucified on Calvary outside the city of Jerusalem. Another difference in these versions of the parable is the escalation of violence. In Matthew two sets of servants are sent (allegorized as the sets of former and latter prophets) and then the son, but in Luke and Mark three individual servants precede the arrival of the son. In Matthew and Mark death comes to a servant before the son; Luke says only that the servants were wounded.

Possibly the most important difference in these versions is in how Jesus phrases his question on guilt. In Mark and Luke Jesus answers the question himself, but in Matthew Jesus forces the Jewish leaders to respond. Thus, Matthew has the chief priests and elders in a way convict themselves, since for the evangelist's audience the allegory of the tenants as representative of Israel's religious hierarchy is clear. Verification of guilt is provided in Matthew, verse 45: "When the chief priests and the Pharisees heard his parables, they realized he was speaking about them."

Context With First And Second Lessons
First Lesson: Isaiah 5:1-7. Isaiah's "Song of the Vineyard" provides the Old Testamant background to Matthew's parable of the wicked tenants. God created a vineyard, Israel, which was given every opportunity to produce a rich harvest, "but it yielded wild grapes." Isaiah, in this first third of his book of prophecy, writes to the people of Judah and predicts their destruction. God nurtured the people, providing everything that was needed, yet the people went their own way and the produce was not satisfactory. The yield of the people was not acceptable to God.

The failure of the Hebrews should have been a warning to the Jews of Jesus' day, but the message was not heeded. God provided the necessary gifts, but the people failed to use them properly; they did not understand or refused to accept their responsibility. Since the gifts were misused they will be taken away and the nation will be destroyed.

Second Lesson: Philippians 3:4b-14. Saint Paul, a former Pharisee and persecutor of the "new way," realized his need for and dependence upon God. All that he possessed was a gift, and thus he could forcefully say to the Philippians that he would give up all for Christ. There is one and only one great prize and that is life with Christ. He realized his need to press forward to achieve this great prize. God would provide what was needed, but Paul understood his responsibility. His cooperation with God's plan was essential. What Paul has is not his own; it is on loan from God and thus must be wisely used.

Paul's exhortation to the Christian community at Philippi must be heeded today. We work hard and feel that personal compensation is our right. We at times lose sight of the one who gave us the opportunity to work. We sometimes as well forget the reasons for the gifts we possess. Paul challenges us to return to a basic understanding that gifts are provided to be properly used; they are not for us alone. Use gifts for God's kingdom and look forward to its realization in our world.

Chapter 11

Perseverance
Brings Us Home

Matthew 22:1-14

---

*Once more Jesus spoke to them in parables, saying, "The
kingdom of heaven may be compared to a king who gave
a wedding banquet for his son. He sent his slaves to call
those who had been invited to the wedding banquet, but
they would not come. Again he sent other slaves, saying,
'Tell those who have been invited: Look, I have prepared
my dinner, my oxen and my fat calves have been slaugh-
tered, and everything is ready; come to the wedding banquet.' But they made light of it and went away, one to his
farm, another to his business, while the rest seized his
slaves, mistreated them, and killed them. The king was
enraged. He sent his troops, destroyed those murderers,
and burned their city. Then he said to his slaves, 'The
wedding is ready, but those invited were not worthy. Go
therefore into the main streets, and invite everyone you
find to the wedding banquet.' Those slaves went out into
the streets and gathered all whom they found, both good
and bad; so the wedding hall was filled with guests.*

*"But when the king came in to see the guests, he no-
ticed a man there who was not wearing a wedding robe,
and he said to him, 'Friend, how did you get in here without a wedding robe?' And he was speechless. Then the
king said to the attendants, 'Bind him hand and foot, and
throw him into the outer darkness, where there will be
weeping and gnashing of teeth.' For many are called,
but few are chosen."*

135

Theme

There is an expression that says "Rome wasn't built in a day." Certainly nothing truly worthwhile or valuable occurs instantaneously. Profitable positions at work, special personal relationships, and achievement of life goals are not completed overnight; they require day-to-day effort and watchfulness. Persistence in all that we do is essential for achievement. Attainment of union with God requires an equal amount of perseverance. We cannot rest assured that our baptism has secured for us a place in God's Kingdom. It is only a start; we must continue to grow, from acceptance of God's initial call to its full realization at the hour of death.

Spiritual Food For The Journey

"If today you do not succeed, try, try again." Great events in human history that were successful on the first try are few and far between, while those which required prolonged effort and multiple attempts predominate. During the era of exploration brave and adventuresome people ventured forth in efforts to discover new lands and people. The discovery and conquest of the New World took a couple hundred years; the task was started in 1492 with Christopher Columbus but was not completed until the cry of Manifest Destiny prompted settlement of the American West. Science has advanced over time through trial and error. Experimentation is the lifeblood of technical advancement. Even something as simple as cooking and baking requires multiple initiatives; the perfect apple pie was not created on the first attempt.

The Christian life requires perseverance and persistence. Our journey to God will not be satisfied with a simple "yes" today to the Lord's call; we must renew our efforts each day in order to maintain our position on the road and not lose our way. In order not to lose sight of the goal we seek there is a need for all Christians to keep their eyes fixed on Jesus and to center ourselves on his message. Vigilance and preparedness for the final call of God is also essential. We may think we have time, but such may not be the case. The great saints were close to God, but it wasn't easy;

they had to work at it daily. Their first efforts at developing a relationship with God were just that — a first attempt. They found God only through perseverance and persistence. We who seek union with God must possess a similar attitude and exercise comparable actions.

The idea of being persistent and doing it consistently must be our attitude of life. God sends us many challenges; we need to be persistent in meeting them. Saint Luke says that the reason Jesus told the parable of the corrupt judge and the widow (18:1-8) was to make a point to his disciples — they were to pray always and never to lose heart. This must be our first lesson in perseverance. We need to spend time in prayer with our God each day. We can make no excuses that we are too busy or time just slipped away. If we are persistent we can make time for prayer. We need to do this, for it is through prayer that we find the strength and the courage to face and overcome the obstacles and difficulties that many times invade, we may even think at times plague, our life.

Another lesson in perseverance comes from the Pastoral epistles. Saint Paul writes to his friend Timothy (2 Timothy 4:2) and tells him, "I solemnly urge you: proclaim the message; be persistent whether the time is favorable or unfavorable; convince, rebuke, and encourage, with the utmost patience in teaching." We encounter many teachers along the road of life. Parents, relatives, mentors, educators, coaches, and others have been given a special ministry to teach. They are to do it whether it is convenient or inconvenient; they are never to lose heart. It is a difficult task to which all who bear the name of Christian are called. It is the perseverance that teachers show that will one day be demonstrated by those to whom they minister.

Let us also remember, however, that we do not take up this often difficult task alone. Baptism calls us to minister to God's people by exercising our faith. In baptism we become children of God. In baptism, also, we become members of a community. That community calls each individual to help the whole group find the unseen God and answer the challenges which come our way. When we work together we can better negotiate the hurdles and obstacles, make straight the crooked paths, and find the hidden way.

Application Of The Parable To Contemporary Life

Sermon Openings
1. He was born to a pious German woman and her Lutheran pastor husband in 1875. With parents of erudition and raised in a Christian environment, it was not unexpected when he began to study theology and philosophy at the university. He was a brilliant student and achieved doctorates in both disciplines by the time he had reached his early twenties. As an academic he was well-known, especially in his immediate purview of colleagues. In 1910, however, he wrote a book, *The Quest for the Historical Jesus*. This was an effort at using historical criticism in application to the gospel narratives. The book made him an international celebrity in theology almost overnight.

At the top of his field, one might think it odd to change direction in life, but God called him to do something different, to dedicate himself to music. As a young man he had toyed with the idea of being a professional musician. Now, as he approached the age of forty, he began to tour the major European cities as a concert organist. His interpretation of the music of Johann Sebastian Bach, both on the concert stage and on some of the first phonographic recordings, was unequaled in his day.

After conquering two different disciplines, theology and musical performance, God again called him to change directions in his life. This time the shift was a radical step — he was called to become a medical missionary in Africa. The challenge would be great, but he went with confidence that all would be provided. French Equatorial Africa had only been "opened" by Christian missionaries a few decades previously. In the 1920s he established a hospital on the Ogoové River in the nation of Gabon. The facility served two functions: as a hospital which met the immediate needs of the local area, and as a leper sanitarium for the greater geographic region.

After laboring for more than thirty years in Africa as a doctor, the world officially recognized the contribution of Albert Schweitzer. In 1952 he was awarded the Nobel Peace Prize. The inscription read, "Granted on behalf of the brotherhood of nations."

Albert Schweitzer accepted several different calls from God. Each required his readiness; each required a certain sense of risk and possibly the need to change. But he went forward, with complete trust, that with God all would be provided.

If God invites, are you ready? This challenging question is posed by today's Gospel. In the parable we hear of God's call, its rejection, and the need always to be ready.

2. On the morning of June 19, 1971, Bill Mitchell was on top of the world. Riding his brand-new motorcycle to a job he loved, gripman on a San Francisco cable car, Bill seemed on cloud nine. Earlier that day he had soloed in an airplane for the first time, the fulfillment of one his fondest dreams. Twenty-eight — handsome, healthy, and popular — Bill was in his element.

In the flash of an eye Bill's whole world changed. Rounding a corner as he neared the cable car barn, Bill collided with a laundry truck. Gas from the motorcycle poured out and ignited through the heat of the engine. Bill emerged from the accident with a broken pelvis and elbow and burns over 65 per cent of his body.

The next six months were a period of great trial for Bill. After several blood transfusions, numerous operations, and many skin grafts, Bill was released from the hospital. Walking down the street he passed a school playground where the children stared at his face. "Look at the monster," they exclaimed. Although he was deeply hurt by the thoughtlessness of the children, he still had the love and compassion of friends and family, and the grace of a good personal philosophy on life. Bill realized that he did not have to be handsome to make a contribution to society. Success was in his hands if he chose to begin again.

Within a year of the accident Bill was moving again toward the success he enjoyed earlier. He began to fly planes. He moved to Colorado and founded a company that built wood stoves. Within no time Bill was a millionaire with a Victorian home, his own plane, and significant real estate holdings.

In November 1975, however, the bottom again fell out of Bill Mitchell's world. Piloting a turbocharged Cessna with four passengers onboard, Bill was forced to abort a take-off, causing the

139

plane to drop about 75 feet like a rock back to the runway. Smoke filled the plane and, fearing that he would again be burned, Bill attempted to escape. Pain in his back and his inability to move his legs thwarted his efforts.

In the hospital again, Bill was informed that his thoracic vertebrae were crushed and the spinal cord was beyond repair. He would spend the rest of his life as a paraplegic. Although doubt began to invade his generally optimistic mind, Bill began to focus on the cans and not the cannots of his life. He decided to follow the advice of the German philosopher Goethe: "Whatever you can do, or dream you can do, begin it. Boldness has genius, power, and magic in it." Before his accidents there were many things Bill could do. He could spend his time dwelling on what was lost or focus on what was left.

Since that 1975 plane accident Bill Mitchell has twice been elected mayor of his town, earned recognition as an environmental activist, and run for Congress. He has hosted his own television show and travels the nation speaking to groups about his message of proper attitude, service, and transformation. Bill's message is to show people that it isn't what happens to you that is important, but what you do about it that makes all the difference.

Bill Mitchell's experience is not typical, but it does present an example of one who triumphed over the greatest of adversities. It was his attitude of perseverance and positive outlook that kept him going, even in the darkest nights of his life. The parable of the wedding guests challenges us to exhibit a similar attitude.

Points Of Challenge And Questions To Ponder

1. Do we accept the invitations extended to us by God? Are we open to the possibility of God in our lives or do we close ourselves off from the challenges God sends our way?

2. The invitation of God may require us to change. Are we flexible enough to alter our schedule and likes and dislikes to accommodate the needs of others?

3. Being children of God is a great privilege. Are we willing to accept and carry out the responsibility that comes with this great privilege? Do we want everything from God without any commitment on our part?

4. How persistent are we to the tasks life brings our way? Do we give up easily? When adversity strikes do we "throw in the towel" and give up?

5. Are we willing to do what is necessary to complete tasks or are we always looking for the easy way out? Do we understand that anything in life of any great value is worthy of our best efforts?

Exegesis And Explanation Of The Parable

The parable of the wedding feast is the last in a series of passages that respond to the challenge brought against Jesus' authority by the religious leaders of the day. These parables were preached during the Lord's last week on earth when he experienced concealed hostility from the Pharisees, chief priests, and elders as they laid traps to catch Jesus in his teaching. Like the other two parables, judgment is the principal idea in this passage, but a noticeable difference exists here with the introduction of judgment on Christians.

Matthew's parable has been viewed by Scripture scholars as an allegory of salvation history. The king is God, the wedding feast represents the Messianic banquet, and those sent to invite the guests are God's prophets, including Christian missionaries. The reference to the mistreatment of the king's slaves recalls the tradition of Israel's violent treatment of God's prophets. The burning of the rebels' city is a reference to the destruction of Jerusalem by the Romans in 70 AD, an event which Christians regarded as God's punishment upon Israel for its rejection of Jesus and the gospel. The invitation offered to others, bad and good, signifies the church's mission to the Gentiles. Matthew's depiction of the wedding feast being prepared for the king's son makes it especially clear that he is thinking of the culmination of salvation history in Jesus. This eschatological feature is most observable when the whole passage, verses 1-14, is examined as a unit.

Although allegory seems adequately to explain the people and events of the parable, this passage is filled with ideas that are totally inconceivable. It is hardly believable that a king would have conformed to the custom of the common citizenry of sending word to invited guests that a banquet was ready. It is possible that a blunt refusal of the invitation may have been given by invited guests, but hardly likely that servants would have been mishandled or killed. It is even more inconceivable that the king would send a second set of slaves when the first are treated so poorly. Why would a king take time to destroy a people and their city when a feast was prepared? Exegetes see verses 6 and 7 to be a later interpolation in the narrative (reference to the 70 AD destruction of Jerusalem) that originally passed from verse 5 to 8.

Matthew's purpose in this parable is at least twofold. First, this pericope illustrates the rejection of Israel and warns the Christian community against the same mistake. The invitation to the banquet is God's call to salvation, but many have refused. For those who reject the call judgment will follow. The assumption has always been that the people want to attend the feast, but when the invitation is extended their unwillingness to follow is revealed. This parable also speaks of preparedness. Devout Jews had decided many centuries before to follow God's lead and to surrender earthly gain, but at the very moment when the invitation to the feast of salvation is extended, the people are not ready. They think there is plenty of time to take care of all things; the feast will come later. Their lack of readiness will cost them the goal they seek. The parable speaks of an invitation to joy, but those invited do not find their way to the feast, while those on the outside are the unexpected guests that were open to the call and have found eternal life.

While some scholars see unity, as introduced above, in verses 1-14, most exegetes divide this pericope into two units: the wedding feast, verses 1-10, and the unworthy guest, verses 11-14. In the first half the failure of Israel to accept God's invitation to salvation as extended by Jesus and the gospel is highlighted. Verses 11-14, however, are a clear admonition to the Christian community to be prepared for the invitation that has now been extended to them. These latter verses reaffirm the original invitation and warning, but they go further and challenge Christians not to be complacent. Scholars suggest that this apparent addition to the original was made by Matthew to dispel false interpretations of the free grace of God. Some people of the day mistakenly held the view that the baptized were free from moral responsibility, because of the reception of God's grace. In order to remove any ground upon which such a misunderstanding could lie, the parable of the unworthy guest was added to the parable of the wedding feast. Matthew thus introduced the principal of merit and emphasized the necessity for repentance as the condition of acquittal at the Last Judgment. Verses 11-14 reflect the self-understanding of the church and its need to adapt messages to actual conditions, including the new missionary activity of the Christian community.

This parable, as it is presented in Matthew, may be a derivative of a Jewish parable of the Rabbi Jochanan (d. 80 AD). In this story a king invited his servants to a feast. The clever ones got dressed up while the foolish ones went about their work. When the feast was suddenly announced, the foolish servants arrived in their working clothes. The king in anger declares, "They shall not eat of my feast." Matthew may have adapted this story in order to achieve his basic end of demonstrating Jesus' authority as well as interjecting an admonition to the community, through the reference to the destruction of Jerusalem. Since the entire structure of chapters 21 through 25 in Matthew's Gospel is an admonition to the Jewish community, it is probable that the evangelist intentionally adopted this Jewish rabbinic tale to demonstrate the need for preparedness in the community for the coming of the Lord.

Some scholars understand verses 11-14 as an allegory that challenges Christians to persevere in conformance to the gospel message. On first examination this pericope is offensive to our sensibilities — why is a poor man so badly treated simply because he does not have the proper clothing? One answer is found if the wedding feast is understood to be the age to come, not the church, and the required garment is righteousness, that is, behavior in accordance with Jesus' teaching. The poor man accepted the invitation, but he refused to conform his life to the gospel. Thus, he is bound hand and foot by servants, representative of God's angels, and cast into the darkness, understood as Gehenna, to wail and grind his teeth.

The parable of the unworthy guest is clearly an illustration of the Last Judgment. The evangelist is demonstrating how it is possible to accept the invitation but not be present. One can be present in body but not in heart and mind. "Called" means merely accepting the initial invitation, but "chosen" asks for perseverance to the end. Those called by God must not look on their invitation as something that is their right. Rather, the call must be renewed each day. When the call no longer shapes one's life or makes it festive, it is removed immediately. The invitation to the banquet must be demonstrated in how one lives life. Matthew is thus exhorting Christians not to lose what they have gained. The summons may come at any time; preparedness is essential to find eternal life.

Context Of The Parable

Context In The Church Year

The parables of the wedding feast and unworthy guest conclude five consecutive weeks of teachings by Jesus. The limitless forgiveness and compassion of God is tempered in these teachings by Jesus' indictment and rejection of Israel and the need for the Christian community as well to be ready when God's call to the feast of eternal life is extended. These teachings as a whole illustrate the privilege and responsibility of the Christian life. God is ever present to show us the correct road and to demonstrate forgiveness and understanding when through sin we remove ourselves from the correct path. But Jesus expects us to do our share; we have responsibility to persevere in rough times and never to abandon the hope and drive that will lead us home to God. Thus, in this week's parable Jesus concludes a lengthy set of lessons that, taken as a whole form, a mini-package of privilege and responsibility as followers of Jesus. We cannot be true disciples unless we are willing to accept God's presence and to participate as fully as we can in building the Kingdom of God in our world.

Context With Other Gospels

The parable of the wedding feast is presented in the Gospels of Luke (14:16-24) and Thomas (Saying 64) as well as Matthew. Scholars believe that Luke and Matthew both utilized the Q source for this parable, for the content and message are the same. Each evangelist, however, uses completely different structures and presents vastly different details. Matthew has embellished the original parable and made it into an allegory for salvation history. In the versions of Luke and Thomas (which parallels Luke closely) there is no mention of a king or that the dinner is a wedding banquet for a son. In these versions the invitation is described briefly, but the excuses rendered by the invited guests are presented with greater detail. Scholars understand the flat refusal of the invitation, as presented in Matthew, as the evangelist's case for Israel's rejection.

Exegetes believe that Luke's version is closest to the original which finds its origins with Jesus. The absence in Luke and Thomas of the parable of the unworthy guest is more evidence that this is a Matthean addition presented to voice the evangelist's warning to the Christian community of its need to continue to persevere throughout and not merely answer the initial call.

Context With First And Second Lessons
First Lesson: Isaiah 25:1-9. The Prophet Isaiah describes a feast provided by God of rich food and choice wines. God will not only provide a great banquet of food, the Lord will wipe away tears and destroy death. Written to the Hebrews before their exile to Babylon, this passage speaks of what God will do for those who persevere and follow the call to holiness. The promise of God was extended through the prophet, but as we know, the invitation to the banquet was not heeded. We will not enjoy the full fruits of God's mercy and compassion unless we are willing to listen and heed God's message. The lesson of the exile should be ample warning for us that action and responsibility must accompany the privilege of faith we share.

145

Second Lesson: Philippians 4:1-9. Saint Paul exhorts the Christian community at Philippi to stand firm in the Lord and to live according to what God has taught us through Jesus Christ. Paul realized from his own experience the difficulty Christians felt in holding fast to what they believed, yet he knew it was imperative for any who wanted to return home to God. The apostle's advice to his friends is to rejoice and to dismiss all anxiety from their minds. In this way it will be easier to find God's peace and to be wholly directed to what is true and deserves respect.

Perseverance in the ways of God is no easier today than in Paul's time. We may not have the threat of persecution, but we have many more outside influences and distractions that draw our attention away from where it should be. Concentrating on God is easier if we can rejoice in the ordinary things we do each day. Rejoicing assists us in our mission to find Christ. We, therefore, must be as joyful as we can and celebrate God's presence in our lives. Such a positive attitude will lead us home one day to union with God.

Chapter 12

Readiness For The Lord

Matthew 25:1-13

---

*"Then the kingdom of heaven will be like this. Ten brides-
maids took their lamps and went to meet the bridegroom.
Five of them were foolish, and five were wise. When the
foolish took their lamps, they took no oil with them; but
the wise took flasks of oil with their lamps. As the bridegroom was delayed, all of them became drowsy and slept.
But at midnight there was a shout, 'Look! Here is the
bridegroom! Come out to meet him.' Then all those
bridesmaids got up and trimmed their lamps. The foolish
said to the wise, 'Give us some of your oil, for our lamps
are going out.' But the wise replied, 'No! There will not
be enough for you and for us; you had better go back to
the dealers and buy some for yourselves.' And while they
went to buy it, the bridegroom came, and those who were
ready went with him into the wedding banquet; and the
door was shut. Later the other bridesmaids came also,
saying, 'Lord, lord, open to us.' But he replied, 'Truly I
tell you, I do not know you.' Keep awake, therefore, for
you know neither the day nor the hour."*

Theme

The motto of the Boy Scouts of America is "Be Prepared."
Preparation is very important in every aspect of life. The better
prepared we are the fewer problems we experience, and those that
come our way are more easily solved. Preparation also leads to
greater acceptance of the hand life deals to us. The more we can

147

think now of future possibilities and prepare ourselves for them, the better able we will be to live and triumph over the pitfalls and struggles of life. Our ultimate preparation must be for the coming of the Lord. Jesus will come when we least expect him. Thus, we must be ready or we will be lost forever.

Spiritual Food For The Journey

Preparation is a constant challenge of life. One might rightly ask the question, "Are we ever truly prepared?" Our life of preparation begins at an early age. In our school days we are specifically preparing ourselves for the future, but each step in the education process is itself preparation for the next step. When we are in elementary school we learn the basics of "the three R's" so that we will be prepared for high school. In this secondary level we work hard and make the grades necessary to prepare ourselves for college or university level work. We might think that we can slack off in college but we realize quickly that the best jobs and placements in graduate school are secured by those who are best prepared.

School is only the beginning of a lifetime of preparation. We prepare through knowledge and experience in our first job for the higher paying and more prestigious position which is our goal. We prepare now our finances for the things we wish to do in the future — vacation, investments, retirement. We formulate plans for our future relationships. Most people hope to find the right person for a lasting, fulfilling, and committed relationship.

Our life is one of constant preparation — are we ever ready? Readiness for a task or event takes much time and preparation. One must be ready to make the sacrifices necessary to assure that the outcome we desire is achieved. Our readiness for God is the most vital of all preparations, for the end we desire will last for eternity. If we in our busy world can take the time to educate ourselves mentally and prepare ourselves physically for events and tasks that are finite, should we not reflect upon the need to make preparations now for the call of the Lord? Some tasks and events come at a prescribed time that makes planning and preparation rather simple. Those that come unannounced require a constant state of readiness. We need to prepare today for Jesus, for as Scripture says, we know not the day nor the hour.

Application Of The Parable To Contemporary Life

Sermon Openings
1. Miracles can happen in the most unusual places. One happened to me in the little town of Trinidad, Colorado, a village of 5,000 people, when everyone is home, in the southeast corner of the state. Trinidad normally serves as a way stop for travelers along I-25, a major north-south route in that part of the country. I was sent to Trinidad in the summer of 1985 to work in a state-run nursing home. There was nothing, I felt, that could possibly be learned from a town with one movie theater, no cultural events, a place where the Greyhound bus stops and departs twice per day. How wrong I could be!

When I arrived I was met by Sr. Mary Theophane, a 79-year-young Sister of Charity. She was to be my mentor during my time in Trinidad. She was a woman full of faith; she was full of energy as well. My first full day of work, Sr. Mary introduced me to all the principals I would need to know, both staff and residents, at the home. That was the day I first met Dr. Hall.

Dr. Hall had been a chiropractor in Trinidad for more than fifty years. Now in retirement, he was living in the home. Dr. Hall was dying, suffering greatly from the pain of bone cancer. I do not remember, if I ever knew, which religious denomination Dr. Hall claimed, but it was obvious to all that he was a Christian man. Dr. Hall lived his life in a state of preparation. He prepared for many different things in varied ways. The first thing for which he prepared was his day. When he felt good he would dress himself; this was his goal. Dr. Hall felt that one should dress properly. For him this meant a long-sleeve shirt, a tie, and a sports jacket. This goal was very precise and he knew just when he had to be ready each day.

There was something else for which Dr. Hall waited — he waited for the presence of God. He knew that God would come to claim him, but he did not know when. How did he prepare for this eventuality? He lived in a spirit of anticipation. He lived filled with joy, despite the pain that was his daily lot. Dr. Hall lived in thanksgiving with the certainty that with every passing day he was one step closer to the goal for which he and all people wait, union with God. Dr. Hall was not afraid or apprehensive. He had no anxiety about an uncertain future. Rather, he lived in a state of patience, and in the process showed many, including myself, the face of God. That was a miracle to me.

Two weeks after I left Trinidad and returned to the novitiate outside Colorado Springs, I received a phone call from my friend Sr. Mary. She informed me of Dr. Hall's death. I thought I should be sad, but rather, I was filled with joy. The one elusive goal for which all people strive, union with God, was now his.

In our busy world we are constantly waiting. We wait in lines, at the bank and at the food store. We wait for our appointment with the dentist or doctor. We wait for special days and celebrations. Most of the events for which we wait have a specific date; we know precisely when they will come. We wait for our birthday, the next three-day weekend, or the next holiday. In each case we know precisely when the event will come. Thus, our preparation can be precise as well. We do not have to be as vigilant as we might. All that we need to do is to complete our list of preparations before the big day. This is the one criterion by which we judge our performance.

There are other events for which we wait which are not as certain in their timing. People in rural areas wait for the rains to nurture the land and crops. In the fall these same people wait for the time of harvest. All people wait for visits from family, friends, and loved ones, events which cannot always be planned. These events require more vigilance. We cannot be lazy; we must develop patience. We all wait for the coming of the Lord at a time that is unknown. We must, therefore, make ourselves ready now for the eventuality down the road.

2. One day a mighty and majestic pine tree, the tallest tree in the whole forest, said to a little squirrel playing in its branches, "There

is a great treasure waiting for you at my topmost branch, if you are willing to make the journey in order to find it." Now this great pine tree was itself a great treasure. It produced some of the meatiest and tastiest pine nuts in the forest and it provided shelter for many animals that called the forest home. This little squirrel was inquisitive, however, and she wondered what the great treasure might be. She decided at that moment to take the journey so as to discover the great treasure.

The trip would be long and because the squirrel was bright she knew planning and preparation were required. Food had to be taken along on the journey. Thus, she chose from her nest some of the best and most delicious nuts that she had stored. She placed them in a little satchel and tied it around her waist. Then she began to climb. At the base of the tree the branches were full and the pine nuts were plentiful, but as she rose higher and higher in the tree, the branches became thinner and thinner and the pine nuts fewer and fewer. She stopped for a moment and rested. She was happy that she had brought food along on the trip. She took out a nut and enjoyed a little snack. This trip was more difficult then she had anticipated. She thought about returning home, but the commitment had been made and she would complete the journey.

As she climbed higher and higher she wondered what the great treasure might be. Maybe she should have asked the tree. But when she looked up she thought she saw the top. There was no need to ask now; she would soon find out for herself. After another half hour of climbing she made it to the top and clung to the topmost branch as it swayed in the wind. She looked around for the treasure, but could see nothing. She thought there might be a giant pine nut or at least one which was delightful to the eye; she saw nothing like this. Had the tree tricked her? Disappointed, frustrated, and now tired and hungry, she prepared to return home. Thus, she turned around, hung upside down, as squirrels often do, and made ready to climb down. But when she looked down the view that she beheld was truly amazing. She could see for miles, every valley and mountain, every stream and river. Because this was the tallest tree in the forest she could see without any obstruction. This was better than any pine nut could possibly be.

She wanted to stay there forever, but realized because the climb had been long and difficult that the sun would set in a few hours and she needed to return home by nightfall. Thus, renewed in spirit, if not in body, she made the easier trip down the tree. That night when speaking to all the other squirrels, she told them about her adventure, and it is said by all her friends that she was never hungry again.[1]

The little squirrel was uncertain as to the great prize, but she knew that it could not be attained without a trip to the top of the tree. That trip required preparation and planning. The gift of eternal life will require an arduous trip for us, but if we do not adequately prepare the gift will never be found.

Points Of Challenge And Questions To Ponder

1. We are constantly preparing for the next event — birthday, anniversary, holiday — but do we take equal care in our preparation for the Lord?

2. Are we procrastinators in our preparation? When it comes to celebrations that are known we might be able to procrastinate, but Jesus will come when we least expect him. Will we be ready?

3. If the headline of the morning paper read, "Jesus Christ To Return Tomorrow!" what would we do? Would we panic, go to church, or run in fear? Could we say we are ready and live with great anticipation of the event?

4. Are we concerned only about our own preparation or do we take time to assist others in their readiness for the Lord? Are we selfish or do we believe that God's call is to all people for all time?

5. Are we sensible in our approach to life? Do we take things as they come and give no care for the future? Do we realize the need for preparation in all things so that we can utilize the gifts and talents we possess to their maximum extent?

Exegesis And Explanation Of The Parable

The parable of the ten virgins presents us with a very confusing picture. While all scholars agree that Matthew is presenting a message on preparedness, they differ greatly on the originality of the parable, its use as an allegory, and its unity. Insufficient knowledge of Palestinian wedding practices and customs has led to much disagreement among exegetes concerning this passage. The parable, recorded only in Matthew, does exhibit the important Matthean theme of the pluralism that exists in the Christian community. The wise and foolish virgins are representative of the wheat and tares (Matthew 13:24-30, 36-43) and the separation of people at the end of time (Matthew 24:40-41, 45-51). Despite the unifying theme and emphasis on pluralism, this passage has been greatly debated in its purpose.

Many scholars believe this parable to be an allegory that explains the second coming of Jesus. By appending the parable to the apocalyptic discourse, exegetes believe that Matthew demonstrates his concern that people be watchful for Jesus' return. Certain details of the story are thus viewed as allegorical. The virgins represent the Christian community that awaits the bridegroom, Jesus the Messiah. This idea is consistent with Matthew's belief that the church is a mixed body, consisting of good and bad, elect and reprobate, wise and foolish. The bridegroom's delay alludes to the fact that Jesus has not returned as soon as many had hoped. The marriage feast symbolizes the life of the age to come. The oil merchants are Moses and the prophets while the call, "Look! Here is the bridegroom," is the trumpet call of God at the return of Christ. The closed doors stand for the Last Judgment. Much disagreement exists on the meaning of the lamps and extra oil. Martin Luther said the oil represented faith; some suggest it is love. The most popular contemporary idea is that the lamps represent good works that must shine before all, while the oil is the Holy Spirit. This latter idea has been challenged, however, as scholars ask if good deeds burn out before the final judgment.

The allegorical interpretation of this parable has gained support from those who point out the unrealistic details of the wedding.

The marriage is described but without mention of the bride. The use of lamps for lighting the way was impractical; torches would have been used. Is it reasonable to think that oil merchants would have been open after midnight for business? The late hour of the wedding and the unexplained delay of the bridegroom also make this passage hard to believe in any way save as allegory. Thus, scholars have labeled the passage as allegory, subsequently attributed to Jesus by the apostolic church, that was intended to exhort the Christian community as the expected Parousia was delayed. The community was challenged not to be negligent in its preparation for the end.

Additional support for the case of allegory is found in the well established use of the feast as an image in Hebrew literature, symbolic of the joys of the Kingdom. The concept of a marriage feast was linked with the theme of the relationship of Yahweh and his people as a marriage. Christianity developed the parallel idea of Christ as the bridegroom and his church as the bride. Thus, the allegorical understanding of the bridegroom as the Messiah reflects not only allegory but provides insight into the Christology of the early church.

The prevailing belief that the parable is an allegory has been challenged by some scholars who suggest that such a conclusion leaves many uncertainties and introduces concepts that were foreign to the period. Exegetes state that the situation presented is not incompatible with the reality of first-century Palestine. Rabbinical material of the period contains only occasional references to marriage customs and there is no indication that the events described in the parable were not customary for the day. The lack of a contemporary description of a wedding in Palestine does not necessarily detract from the originality of the story. Additionally, there are parallels between the events in the parable and modern Palestinian village customs, such as the reception of a bridegroom with lamps, the celebration of weddings at night, and even the late arrival of the bridegroom. Some scholars suggest as well that the allegory of the Messiah as a bridegroom is completely foreign to the whole of the Old Testament and to the literature of Judaism of the period. Thus, the passage has been described by some biblical exegetes as a story of what preceded an actual wedding.

The question of origin of the parable necessitates some review of its possible connection with Jesus. Some scholars have argued that the original parable of Jesus is at the core of the pericope. The key question is whether the details are realistic, which would label the passage as a parable, or contrived to fit the theological understanding of the writer, leading to the conclusion of allegory. Some scholars suggest the midnight hour as one key element. If the idea of midnight generically means that there has been a delay, then the events described could be real, and thus the parable be original to Jesus. If, on the other hand, the hour of midnight is specific and essential to the story, then the pericope probably originated as an allegory with the Christian community, which realized that Jesus was not returning as soon as was first expected. Certain Scripture experts see this passage as a mutilated form of an authentic parable of Jesus. In other areas of the New Testament Jesus warned his disciples that foes would be present in the Kingdom, even within one's own household (Matthew 10:34-36), that loyalty to lesser causes and to God were not compatible (Matthew 10:37-38 and Luke 9:57-62), and that discriminations in those chosen would be inevitable. Some will be taken and others left (Luke 17:33-35).

The message of the pericope, whether it is viewed as allegory or parable, is preparedness for the coming of the Lord. As the coming of the bridegroom in the parable finds some attendants insufficiently prepared, the arrival of the Kingdom, with the Parousia and the Son of Man, will find some professed Christians unready. If they have not made the necessary preparations while there was time, there will be no opportunity to make up for lax attitudes and slack behavior at the last moment. Readiness in Matthew means living the life of the Kingdom by carrying out the precepts of the Sermon on the Mount. Many can do this for a short while, but when the Kingdom is delayed, problems arise. Being a peacemaker for a day is not as demanding as being a peacemaker year after year when hostility breaks out again and the bridegroom is delayed. Being merciful for an evening is pleasant, but being merciful for a lifetime, when the groom is delayed, requires preparedness. The obvious teaching is that those who fail to do the will of God and are not prepared for his return will be excluded from the Kingdom of Heaven. The attempt to buy oil after the arrival of the bridegroom demonstrates the futility of trying to prepare when it is too late. When the doors are shut there will no longer be an opportunity for repentance. God's judgment will be unequivocal and irreversible. Thus, the necessary preparations must be made.

Verse 13 of this passage is probably not part of the original parable since its message of vigilance is not the main point of the story. Nothing in the parable indicates that the bridesmaids were expected to stay awake. The wise as well as the foolish virgins fell asleep while they were waiting. Watchfulness is, therefore, not the outstanding characteristic that is taught in this parable. Rather, it is the quality of the preparation that is accented. This teaching was directed to Jesus' followers, the rank and file, as well as Jewish leaders. As the bridegroom in the time and culture of Jesus came late and without notice, so Jesus will arrive suddenly. Matthew wants the people to be ready for the Parousia when it comes.

Context Of The Parable

Context In The Church Year

For the final three weeks of the liturgical year the church turns to Matthew chapter 25 and its message of the Second Coming and God's judgment. For the next three weeks we will hear parables which demonstrate how God will make decisions on who will enter the Kingdom of Heaven and who will be barred. As the church begins to close one liturgical year and prepare for the season of Advent, we need to be reminded not only that there will be a final judgment, but also what the criteria for entry will be. Today, in the first of three parables, we are told of the general need for preparation. Jesus' return has been delayed; his arrival is uncertain. We can watch with great vigilance, but if we are not ready we will find ourselves on the outside. The Kingdom will come; we, however, must prepare now or be lost forever.

Context With Other Gospels

Matthew has skillfully placed this pericope after Jesus' discourse on the end times. In the last part of that discourse Jesus speaks of a division between those who are chosen, alert, and faithful, and those who are not. "Then two [men] will be in the field; one will be taken and one will be left. Two women will be grinding meal together; one will be taken and one will be left" (24:40-41). The faithful and wise servant is placed in charge of all his master's possessions, but the wicked servant is assigned a place with the hypocrites (24:45-51). Thus, in the parable of the ten virgins, five enter the bridegroom's house and five find the door locked. This theme of separating the good from the bad is continued in the parable of the talents (25:14-30) and the description of a shepherd separating sheep from goats (24:31-33).

While this parable is found only in Matthew, there are some passages in Scripture which echo some of the ideas present in the story of the ten virgins. Luke 13:25-28 speaks of the door being locked, stopping access to the house. The admonition to keep watch is found in the conclusion of the Markan discourse, 13:33-37.

Context With First And Second Lessons
First Lesson: Amos 5:18-24 or Wisdom 6:12-16. The prophet Amos wrote to the Northern Kingdom of Israel in the eighth century before Christ. He portrays a dark image of the day of the Lord. The faithlessness of the Hebrews in the North will bring ruin to them before they know it. Amos forecasts the destruction of the kingdom at a time that will come swiftly and without warning. He calls the day of the Lord darkness, a clear indication that God's wrath rather than blessing will fall upon the people.

Amos' prophecy was a warning to the Northern Kingdom of its fate, but it became a lesson for the Hebrews centuries later of what can happen to those who are unprepared. The message for us is the same. We all think that we have infinite time, and thus many times we fail to make the necessary preparations today for the coming of the Lord. Amos spoke God's word, but his message was ignored. Thus, God's judgment came swiftly and severely against the Northern Kingdom. We are challenged to heed the warning today so our fate will not be the darkness of death, but the light of eternal salvation.

157

Second Lesson: 1 Thessalonians 4:13-18. Saint Paul presents a message of hope to the Christian community at Thessalonica. Many feared that those who died before the Parousia would be lost, but Paul is clear in his teaching that those who are living will have no advantage over the dead when the Lord returns. Since the day of Jesus' return is not known there is a great need for preparation, but such effort is not wasted should one die.

Paul is confident that Jesus will return and those who have made preparations will be joined with him. This is a much more consoling message than the gloom prophesied by Amos. The Apostle to the Gentiles tells his readers that they must console each other with the message that Jesus' salvation can be theirs. Similarly, we need only be ready to accept it when it is offered.

---

1. Paraphrased from "The Squirrel and the Pine Tree," in John R. Aurelio, *Colors! Stories of the Kingdom* (New York: The Crossroad Publishing Company, 1993), pp. 63-64.

Chapter 13

God's Gifts
Are For All

Matthew 25:14-30

*"For it is as if a man, going on a journey, summoned his
slaves and entrusted his property to them; to one he gave
five talents, to another two, to another one, to each according to his ability. Then he went away. The one who
had received the five talents went off at once and traded
with them, and made five more talents. In the same way,
the one who had the two talents made two more talents.
But the one who had received the one talent went off and
dug a hole in the ground and hid his master's money. After
a long time the master of those slaves came and settled
accounts with them. Then the one who had received the
five talents came forward, bringing five more talents, saying, 'Master, you handed over to me five talents; see, I
have made five more talents.' His master said to him,
"Well done, good and trustworthy slave; you have been
trustworthy in a few things, I will put you in charge of
many things; enter into the joy of your master.' And the
one with the two talents also came forward, saying, 'Master, you handed over to me two talents; see, I have made
two more talents.' His master said to him, 'Well done,
good and trustworthy slave; you have been trustworthy in
a few things, I will put you in charge of many things; enter
into the joy of your master.' Then the one who had received the one talent also came forward, saying, 'Master,
I knew that you were a harsh man, reaping where you did
not sow, and gathering where you did not scatter seed; so*

159

I was afraid, and I went and hid your talent in the ground. Here you have what is yours.' But his master replied, 'You wicked and lazy slave! You knew, did you, that I reap where I did not sow, and gather where I did not scatter? Then you ought to have invested my money with the bankers, and on my return I would have received what was my own with interest. So take the talent from him, and give it to the one with the ten talents. For to all those who have, more will be given, and they will have an abundance; but from those who have nothing, even what they have will be taken away. As for this worthless slave, throw him into the outer darkness, where there will be weeping and gnashing of teeth.' "

Theme

Gifts are given to be enjoyed and utilized. Gifts are chosen and presented because the giver believes the receiver can effectively use the present for work, relaxation, or self-improvement. We only give to those we love gifts which we feel can be beneficial to them. God has provided us with many and varied gifts, but they have been provided only in the measure that we can effectively use them. God gave us gifts so that we could make the world a better place, not only for ourselves, but for all people. The parable of the talents challenges us to reflect upon our actions so that the gifts we have been given by God can be best used to build the Kingdom today and to eternal life.

Spiritual Food For The Journey

All of us, we who are God's children, have been entrusted with many gifts. Are we using them effectively? We have all been given a certain amount of responsibility. It may come in the form of decisions that we make; it may come in the position that we hold. Sometimes responsibility is shown in being an advocate for another, whether that be in the community, at work, or in the church.

All of us as well have been entrusted with the care of others. Parents have been entrusted with the care of their children, to love,

160

nurture, and to raise with Christian values. Husbands and wives have been given to each other. Teachers have been given their students to educate and encourage. Doctors, lawyers, and other professionals have been given their clients.

We have all been entrusted with many possessions. It may be money or other securities. It may be material items such as a car, a home, clothes — all that we have. We have also been entrusted with our own personal talents. For one person the gift may be intelligence, for another it may be the ability to speak or listen well. Others may be gifted in artistic expression, such as music or painting. Still others will be gifted in the area of athletics and sports.

In short, we have been entrusted with our very lives. The gifts we have, the responsibilities we have been given, the people entrusted to us are given by God, but only in the measure that we are able to use them. How are we doing with our use of the gifts given to us? Are others as well as ourselves able to benefit from these gifts? Do we believe that although the world extols and magnifies the beautiful and outward, it may be the latent or unseen talent, if allowed to blossom forth, that can produce the greatest yield?

God calls us to responsibility for the gifts we have been given. As Scripture says, more will be asked of the one to whom more is given. But remember, we have been given only what we have the ability to use. God is certain we can rightly use and care for the gifts, possessions, and people we have — that is precisely why they were given to us! Let us search our minds, our hearts, our very being, and see how we can better use God's gifts, especially the one that may be latent or less visible. Let all that we are and all that we do give greater glory to God and all God's people.

Application Of The Parable To Contemporary Life

Sermon Openings
1. Peter and Hans were best friends. Growing up together they were truly inseparable. Whether it was playing ball, studying their lessons, or going to church, these two best friends did things together. Their families were close as well. They lived in the same

neighborhood; they associated freely. Peter and Hans were gifted young men, but each in a different way. Peter's gifts were more open and visible. Hans was able to attain the same heights of accomplishment as Peter, but he had to do it with gifts that were less obvious and more hidden. Hans had to work harder than Peter for the same result. As well as being gifted both boys felt they had a call, a vocation to the ministry.

The village where the boys lived held an academic competition each year. The prize was a scholarship to the seminary located in the provincial capital. When Peter and Hans finished their preparatory education they entered the competition. Each was severely tested, as were all the other candidates. The results, as might be expected, were a dead heat with Peter and Hans at the head of the list. The village elders did not think it right to choose one boy over the other. Thus, this one year they made an exception and awarded two scholarships with the proviso that after one year the boys' performance would be evaluated.

After spending the summer months in the village Peter and Hans left together on the train for the provincial capital. When they arrived at the seminary the best friends began to separate for the first time in their lives. Peter, the one whose talents were more visible, adapted well to his new environment. He integrated himself into the seminary routine. He made many new friends. He had been entrusted with many gifts. He had his own personal talents, but there was the scholarship and most especially the confidence of the people back home. Peter was determined to demonstrate that the many gifts he possessed could yield more in the end. Hans, on the other hand, did not adapt well. He did not integrate himself into the seminary life. He had been entrusted with a variety of gifts, as had Peter, yet he felt no need to gain anything more. His gifts remained hidden where they did little good.

The day of reckoning came for both boys. After one year the village elders wanted to know how their prize students had progressed. Peter had done well. His professors and others responsible for his formation gave him high praise. The gifts he brought had yielded a bountiful harvest. Hans, however, had not done well. In fact, he was close to failure in his classes and he was

162

not appreciated by those in charge of his performance. The elders acted as they saw fit. Peter was retained and given an extension on his scholarship; Hans' scholarship was revoked. The little that he had was taken and given to one who had shown greater potential and initiative.

Thus begins the novel *Beneath the Wheel*, one of the lesser known but nonetheless wonderful stories by Hermann Hesse, the well-known German writer. It is a story of gifts given, gifts abused, and ultimately gifts taken away. The story of Peter and Hans closely parallels the parable told by Jesus in today's Gospel. The wealthy owner possesses many talents and wants to share them with his servants, but only in the measure that each servant is able to use them.

2. There is an ancient Asian tale which describes the difference between heaven and hell. The image of hell, so says the tale, begins with the description of a long banquet-like table around which many are seated, preparing to eat. The meal is ready, abundant, and on the table. The scene seems pretty normal except the silverware — each utensil is three feet long. In observing the scene we see that nothing is happening; nobody is eating. Instead of eating, all of those at table are fighting with each other. The utensils are so big that one cannot feed him or herself. Chaos is the result.

The image of heaven begins with the same banquet table. The meal is prepared; the people are present. Again the silverware utensils are three feet long. All in heaven are eating, however. These people have learned that the only way they can eat is by feeding each other. Mutual cooperation allows all to be fed.

This Asian tale says something very powerfully, I think, about our modern world and society. It seems to say that individual pursuit will land you in the wrong place. The tale tells us about the differences between those who find total fulfillment and satisfaction in self, as opposed to those who find fulfillment and satisfaction in God. Our world places many temptations in our path. There is the temptation to self-indulgence from food, drink, or drugs. There is the temptation to total self-satisfaction in work or sport. There is also the temptation to complete self-reliance, the idea that we have no need for others. It is the mentality that says I can do it all myself. Such individual pursuit is the Asian image of hell.

The parable of the talents suggests that we must properly use the gifts given to us by God. Since all is a gift from God, we must use our talents, resources, and time to better the whole of society and not merely our own pursuits.

Points Of Challenge And Questions To Ponder

1. How effectively do we use the gifts given us by God? Who gains the most benefit from them — ourselves or others?

2. Are we wasteful in the manner we use the things of the world? Do we realize that all is a gift that originates from God?

3. Are we complacent in our lives? Do we wait for others to act before we make our move? Do we wish others to do things for us or do we take the initiative to help them?

4. Do we act as if God or the world owed us something? Do we seek our own comfort and security over that of the community?

5. God has given us our lives for service to the Lord and to all men and women. We are provided gifts in the measure we are able to use them effectively. Have we done our best with what God has provided or have we shirked our responsibilities?

Exegesis And Explanation Of The Parable

The parable of the talents is the third in a series of passages in Matthew that focus on judgment. In the first, the parable of the master and servant (24:45-51), the evangelist focuses on the accountability of church leaders; in the second, the parable of the ten bridesmaids (25:1-13), emphasis is placed on the responsibilities of all Christians. The parable of the talents speaks to those with obligations from special gifts that have been granted. It is routine for Christians to excuse themselves through the rationalization that their gifts are too modest to be significant. This parable asserts the gifts are valuable and are to be utilized to their fullest extent.

The question of allegory, as with most parables, has been discussed by scholars in efforts to understand this pericope. Most scholars view the passage as an allegory that was written to deliver the message that Christians must be active and exercise opportunity when it comes before the return of Christ. Matthew has used the Q source parable, rewriting it to serve his purpose of describing the active nature of the Christian life as we await Christ's return. The evangelist is concerned that believers not only hear the message but transform what they hear into action; Jesus' disciples are to keep busy in their master's absence. Scripture exegetes suggest that Matthew's use of a talent, an immense sum of money equivalent to fifteen years' pay for a common laborer, is intended to remind readers of the precious nature of God's gifts. The fact that the slaves are given different amounts represents the various gifts from God, not something equally shared by all Christians, such as the gospel. Understood as allegory, the merchant becomes a symbol for Christ, the journey his ascension, and his subsequent return the Parousia which ushers some into the Messianic banquet and casts others into the darkness. Christ is shown as the judge of all whose rewards are not simple, but rather bring one to heavenly joy, and whose punishments are not simply rebukes for failure to exercise opportunity, but condemnation. The eschatological nature of the parable is evident in two ways. Verses 21 and 23, "enter into the joy of your master," and verse 30, "throw him into the outer darkness," show Christ of the Parousia who awards a share in the New Age to some and assigns others to eternal damnation.

While most experts understand the parable of the talents as allegory, there are others who believe it to be dangerous and irrelevant to allegorize the passage. Some exegetes suggest that the pericope can be read as a story of normal happenings. It is believable that one who entrusts others with valuable property should expect some return from the trust placed in those who serve as guardians. One expectation would govern the treatment of the servants and the nature of the reward or punishment. Understanding the pericope as a story makes the characterization of the merchant more rational. With the first two servants the merchant is merciful, but with the last he is harsh. Some suggest that such a characterization of Christ makes him appear inconsistent, whereas such behavior would be totally understandable from one whose trust had been rejected by a servant who showed no initiative.

The basic teaching of the parable of the talents is that every believer has been entrusted by God with gifts, provided according to one's ability, that must be used in the Lord's service. Gifts provided must be used now. The lengthy absence of the master makes it possible for the slaves to be entrusted with real responsibility in the interim. Two of the slaves take a risk which could entail the loss of everything entrusted to them, because they understood that what their master gave them must be actively used; it must live and effect something new. For some time the situation is constant, but eventually the day of reckoning comes. The slaves who risk are rewarded with more responsibility. The message is clear: the person who is ready to extend and risk one's life will find it, not the one who wishes to secure it.

Although the parable speaks of the reward for the first two slaves, far more attention is given to the negative example and disastrous fate of the third slave. The slave rationalizes his failure by blaming the master, whom he describes as a harsh man. He appears to be interested only in himself and, consequently, security and not service is his goal. There is no indication of gratitude that the master entrusted him with so great a sum. Rather, the slave sees the master's gift as a just due with which he can secure himself. If it is correct to interpret verse 15, "to each according to his ability," as indicating that for Matthew the parable challenges Christians to make full use of gifts that God has entrusted to them, then the portrayal of the third slave reminds us that love for our master, God, must be demonstrated in faithful and untiring service to others. In his absence Jesus' followers are expected to work diligently with the gifts entrusted to them; they will be held accountable on the day of his return.

The parable of the talents is directed toward those devoted to their own personal security and vindication of their own righteousness, rather than committed to God, which means devoted to others. Those that are anxious about their own continuance and fail to notice that this anxiety is causing them to let the gifts of God lie dormant, or who think themselves to be right and accuse God of injustice, like the day laborer (Matthew 20:12) or the elder (unforgiving) brother of the parable of the prodigal son (Luke 15:29-30) have committed the error of the third slave. More generically Jesus is saying that a religion concerned only with doing nothing wrong in order that its practitioners may one day stand vindicated ignores the will of God.

Some debate exists as to whom the parable was originally addressed. When Jesus' disciples initially heard these words they may have thought the parable applied to Israel and its Jewish contemporaries. Some nations have many interests, but Israel had only one concern — spreading the revelation of God. The Lord expected Israel to take responsibility for the gifts entrusted to it. God gave the Jews his work and he expected that they would make his revelation known everywhere. Jesus' disciples might have seen the law-abiding Pharisee and teacher of the law personified in the servant who buried the one talent. The religious leaders of Israel were entrusted with a sacred deposit of revelation, but many of them failed to put it to proper use. They kept the deposit for themselves; they failed to put it to work. God, who gave the gift, would one day ask for an accounting.

Other scholars suggest that the parable was originally intended for Jesus' disciples. Entrusted with the gift of the gospel, the apostles were commissioned to go forth and proclaim the message throughout the world. This parable has spoken to Christians through the centuries, as it does today, of the need to share God's revelation with those around us. Thus, the parable serves to illustrate Jesus' challenge to be good disciples.

Context Of The Parable

Context In The Church Year
Today's celebration is the second of three consecutive readings from chapter 25 of Matthew where the evangelist describes the criteria for judgment. Last week preparedness was the key;

next week the specific criteria for salvation will be explained. Today we are told of the importance of utilizing our gifts in the pursuit of God's kingdom. As the liturgical year draws to a close we are encouraged to look at our lives and reflect upon what we have been given and our responsibilities to God for those gifts. So many times the gifts become the center of our lives and the giver is forgotten. We need to be reminded that such an attitude is inconsistent with the Christian call. We are to use the gifts of God to assist God's people and to build the Kingdom in our world.

Context With Other Gospels

The parable of the talents is found in various forms in the Gospel of Luke (19:11-27) and the apocryphal text, the Gospel of the Nazarenes. Scholars generally agree that the oldest form of the parable and that which most closely resembles Jesus' words is that of Matthew. One reason for this conclusion is that there are indications in Luke that there were originally only three servants (versus ten) and to them graduated responsibilities were given. The Lukan version, the parable of the pounds, is a variant of Matthew's story, drawn most probably from the same Q source. Several important differences in the two versions exist. In Luke the distribution of the goods is not made according to ability, but with a view to testing one's capacity. In Luke the slaves are given a mere fraction of what they receive in Matthew, and those who are successful are rewarded with responsibility rather than more gifts. One important similarity is that both evangelists say that something must be done by Christians before the Parousia.

Some scholars suggest that the two parables are actually different. Based on the setting and historical framework of the two pericopes, plus the scope of the parables, some exegetes believe that Jesus taught these two parables separately.

The Gospel of the Nazarenes, a second-century Targum of Matthew's Gospel, provides the third version. In this form one servant multiplies the capital, one hides it, and one squanders it with harlots and flute players. The first is rewarded, the second rebuked, and the third is cast into prison. This version, by the fact that it is in some ways is more satisfying to our moral and aesthetic sense, is further removed from the original story of Jesus, which was more upsetting to our idea of justice.

Some see the parable of the talents as a further variation of the seminal Marcan parable of the servants awaiting the Lord's return (Mark 13:32-37). A strong similarity in the beginnings of these passages leads some to conclude that in setting up the parable Matthew is following Mark. The former goes beyond Mark, however, in describing the need for activity in the interim of the master's absence.

Context With First And Second Lessons
First Lesson: Zephaniah 1:7, 12-18. Zephaniah wrote to the people of Judah in the seventh century BC before the Babylonian exile. The prophet preached against religious degradation, which was common in his day. In this reading he speaks of The Day of the Lord as a future disaster of overwhelming proportion. Zephaniah says that God will "punish the people who rest complacently on their dregs, those who say in their hearts, 'The Lord will not do good, nor will he do harm' " (1:12b).

Zephaniah's message prophesied that complacency would lead to destruction for the Hebrews. Jesus' message in the parable of the talents is very similar. We must be willing to take the risks necessary to utilize fully the gifts God has entrusted to us. If we rest and are complacent, the little we have will be taken away and given to the one with initiative. Our destruction will follow.

Second Lesson: 1 Thessalonians 5:1-11. Saint Paul's belief in the imminent nature of the Second Coming of Christ is a major theme of his two letters to the Thessalonians. Paul's warning to the people that Christ will come when they least expect him mandates that they not be caught off guard. The Thessalonians are encouraged to be awake and sober. Christians are to live day by day in the sure and certain hope of salvation.

Paul's words support Jesus' message of the need for action as people wait for Christ's return. If people are complacent and live in total peace with no thoughts of others, the end will come without warning and there will be no escape. Action, vigilance, and preparation are all part of Paul's message to the Thessalonians.

Chapter 14

Serving Christ
Through Others

Matthew 25:31-46

---

*"When the Son of Man comes in his glory, and all the
angels with him, then he will sit on the throne of his glory.
All the nations will be gathered before him, and he will
separate people one from another as a shepherd separates the sheep from the goats, and he will put the sheep
at his right hand and the goats at his left. Then the king
will say to those at his right hand, 'Come, you that are
blessed by my Father, inherit the kingdom prepared for
you from the foundation of the world; for I was hungry
and you gave me food, I was thirsty and you gave me
something to drink, I was a stranger and you welcomed
me, I was naked and you gave me clothing, I was sick and
you took care of me, I was in prison and you visited me.'
Then the righteous will answer him, 'Lord, when was it
that we saw you hungry and gave you food, or thirsty and
gave you something to drink? And when was it that we
saw you a stranger and welcomed you, or naked and gave
you clothing? And when was it that we saw you sick or in
prison and visited you?' And the king will answer them,
'Truly I tell you, just as you did it to one of the least of
these who are members of my family, you did it to me.'
Then he will say to those at his left hand, 'You that are
accursed, depart from me into the eternal fire prepared
for the devil and his angels; for I was hungry and you
gave me no food, I was thirsty and you gave me nothing
to drink, I was a stranger and you did not welcome me,*

*naked and you did not give me clothing, sick and in prison
and you did not visit me.' Then they will also answer,
'Lord, when was it that we saw you hungry or thirsty or a
stranger or naked or sick or in prison, and did not take
care of you?' Then he will answer them, 'Truly I tell you,
just as you did not do it to one of the least of these, you
did not do it to me.' And these will go away into eternal
punishment, but the righteous into eternal life."*

Theme

A popular Christian hymn starts, "Whatsoever you do to the
least of my brothers, that you do unto me." Service to others has
always been an integral part of the Christian message. For centuries men and women, famous and unknown, have carried out Jesus'
dictate to love by caring for the needs and desires of others. In
Matthew's depiction of the Last Judgment we are challenged to
see the face of Christ in all and to render service to them as we
would to the Lord himself. Kindness done to a person in need will
bring not only a warmth in our hearts, it is one of the criteria used
by God to determine our eternal fate. May we respond to the needs
of our sisters and brothers and in the process meet Jesus face to
face.

Spiritual Food For The Journey

When I was in the fifth grade or thereabouts, as I best recall,
there was a popular song on the radio, "Love Is Just a Four-Letter
Word." The song was written and sung by Joan Baez, a well-
known folk singer in the 1960s. In the lyrics of the song, Ms. Baez
tried to show that love, although it has only four letters, and therefore might be thought by some to a simple word because it is so
short, is in reality a very complex concept. All of us through life
experience know that love is a very involved idea.

The ancient Greeks, a highly intelligent and civilized people,
also realized that love was a complicated idea. Among the many
gifts that the Greeks gave us was the study of philosophy, the science of thought. In philosophy and in language, the Greeks used

three different words to express adequately the multiple concepts of love. The first type of love for the Greeks was *phileo*. This is brotherly and sisterly love. It is the type of love expressed between siblings, the love shared with a best friend. This is certainly a special form of love and highly expressive in our world. The second word the Greeks used to express love was *eros*. This is romantic love, the love between one man and one woman. This type of love is centered in self. Although we may give much to the one we love in such a way, *eros* is an emotion which is self-satisfying, a personal need that all people feel and desire. The third form, and for the Greeks the highest form of love, is *agapao*, commonly known as agape. This is the love we outwardly express in our service, ministry, and relations with others. Agape is centered on the other, not the self. It is, therefore, a special and powerful love which is rooted in the Christian understanding of faith and Jesus' message of love and service.

Service, for the Greeks the highest form of love, must be an integral part of our everyday lives. It is easy to say, I am too busy, I don't have the expertise, or I don't have the resources to assist. These are simply excuses which do not erase the Christian responsibility we have to serve others. Jesus came to serve, not to be served. If we wish to walk in the footsteps of the Lord, then we cannot shirk our duties to others. Let us demonstrate love by being people of service, assisting others, and in the process building God's Kingdom on earth.

Application Of The Parable To Contemporary Life

Sermon Openings
1. The call came one day in a subtle and very quiet way. There was a knock on the door to a Lower East Side Manhattan apartment. It was December, 1932. The nation was mired in the Great Depression; unemployment and poverty were everywhere. The man who knocked at the door wore baggy pants and a tattered coat; he was unshaven. The man who came to the door that day was a visionary named Peter Maurin; he had come to visit Dorothy Day. As an immigrant to the United States from France, Maurin had

personally experienced the depths of despair in which many people presently found themselves. His solution was threefold: roundtable discussions where the issues of the day could be debated and solutions sought, farming communes where community could be built and appreciated, and houses of hospitality where the poor could be serviced with dignity. Peter Maurin had a vision which required a person of action.

The knock on the door that December morning was the answer to a prayer for Dorothy Day. Dorothy had worked as a journalist for radical newspapers in New York; she had been searching for the elusive vocation which is the desire of all women and men. Her journey had been difficult; poverty, a short-lived marriage, and an abortion had been her experience. Yet, Dorothy had found Catholicism, was now a mother, and needed a way to implement the God-given gifts she possessed. In the call from Peter Maurin she found where she must go.

God's call for Dorothy Day became concrete that December day. She was able to combine her ability to write and her need for action with the ideas of Peter Maurin to form a new movement, the Catholic Worker. It began as a one cent per copy newspaper first issued on May Day, 1933, in Union Square, New York. It grew into many houses of hospitality, which fed and sheltered the poor and marginal of society, in Manhattan and other major metropolitan areas. Later a farming commune was established outside Easton, Pennsylvania, to encourage community life and prayer. The Catholic Worker became for Dorothy Day and many women and men who followed her lead a passion, a way of life. The Catholic Worker still lives today in many American cities. The knock on the door that day changed Dorothy Day forever. For her it was a call to holiness, her call to discipleship.

Dorothy Day's life, recently depicted in a motion picture, *Entertaining Angels*, models the understanding of Christian service, especially to those who are poor, weak, and marginalized in society — the least of our brothers and sisters. Matthew's apocalyptic drama of the sheep and the goats challenges us to lead lives of service as the main criterion for eternal life.

2. The Black experience of Christians in the United States, especially Roman Catholics, has been one of much pain and anguish. Often denied the opportunity to worship and certainly the freedom to freely exercise their faith as they chose, it is almost inconceivable that a former slave would rise to success and fame through his service to others. Yet, this is exactly the story of Pierre Toussaint, a man who is little known to history, but one whose inspiring story should be heard by all.

Toussaint was born into slavery in the French colony of Dominique, now Haiti, in 1766. The plantation owner where Pierre lived was a devout Catholic who treated his slaves in a relatively humane manner. When he was 21, Toussaint came with his owner to the newly-established United States and settled in New York City. When his owner suddenly died, Toussaint found himself in the odd position of having financially to support himself and his owner's widow, who was penniless. Having been taught the elements of hairdressing, Toussaint was able to earn enough money to support all in his care. Because of his loyalty, Toussaint was given his freedom in 1807. Later he was able to purchase the freedom of his sister and a second woman, Mary Rose Juliette, whom he married in 1811.

Toussaint's economic success as a hairdresser did not mean that he avoided the prejudice of the day. As a black among Catholics and a Haitian among blacks he was a minority within each of these minorities. Even though he was a pewholder in St. Peter's Church, the oldest Catholic parish in New York, he felt the scourge of racial prejudice from many Catholics in the city. Many objected to the presence of him and his wife in the congregation. Toussaint took the slight in stride as a necessary evil of the day.

Pierre Toussaint was a generous benefactor of many church projects in New York. He economically supported the Catholic Orphan asylum of New York and regularly assisted St. Vincent de Paul Church, the first French parish in the city. Though he and his wife remained childless, they took into their home many destitute black children whom they sheltered and educated until they were able to fend for themselves. Daily after attending church services, Toussaint walked the streets of the city, aiding the poor by meeting the needs that they faced. His charity and piety became known throughout the city. Until his death in June 1853, he remained a man of peace and service to all in need. In 1997 he was declared venerable, the first stage in Roman Catholicism on the path to canonization.

Pierre Toussaint overcame the prejudice and evil of society in providing loving service to many in the city of New York. He stands as an outstanding example of Jesus' exhortation in today's Gospel to serve those who are our least brothers and sisters, for through such action we serve the Lord Himself.

Points Of Challenge And Questions To Ponder

1. God's call as evidenced by the story of sheep and goats is one of action. How much effort do we make to assist others? What kind of priority does service rate in our lives?

2. Do we take the time that is necessary to be with people or are we too "tied up" with our own lives? Do we find the needs of others to be an intrusion in our lives?

3. When we encounter a person on the street who needs our assistance, what has been our response in the past? Have we assisted or walked by? What has been our attitude?

4. Do we hear the cry of the poor throughout the world? Are we too comfortable in our first-world environment to look outside ourselves and see the needs that face most of the world's inhabitants?

5. Can we perceive the reality of social sin in our nation and world? Do we notice unjust practices in business or government that keep some at a disadvantage while extending privileges to others?

Exegesis And Explanation Of The Parable

Most scholars believe that Matthew 25:31-46, the so-called parable of the sheep and goats, is an apocalyptic drama of the Last

Judgment. This pericope is the final scene in a series of judgment passages (24:42—25:46) that the evangelist uses to close Jesus' apocalyptic discourse. The parables of the thief, servant, wise and foolish virgins, and talents are capped by this passage of the Last Judgment. Most Scripture exegetes fail to see in this pericope the basic form of parable, namely, where a familiar scene of the world is moderated to a new dimension of meaning. This passage, in contrast, begins with an otherworldly depiction of the Parousia — the coming of the Son of Man with his angels and the gathering of nations before the throne — then modulates into affirmation of the importance of everyday worldly deeds. Scholars differ on their understanding of the passage's origins, but it is almost universally agreed that the pericope is not a parable in the strict sense of the term.

It has been customary to interpret this passage in universal terms where all people will be judged based on how they have treated the needy and distressed of the world. This understanding, while providing a needed corrective that places a high priority on service to the poor, is plagued with problems. First, the principal teaching of the story is not strictly Christian. Ancient Egyptians, for example, believed that good deeds would win them life after death. Thus, the Christian doctrine of faith appears to play no role. Those saved have done their good deeds without any apparent thought that they were serving Christ. The pericope also lacks any reference to the doctrine of the forgiveness of sins or the grace of God. The righteous are invited to enter into the Kingdom because they have shown themselves worthy by deed, not because their sins are forgiven. There is no mercy for the accursed and the blessed have no need for mercy. There is justice for all, but scholars have suggested that justice without mercy is not Christian in nature. Another difficulty with this pericope is that it ignores suggestions from earlier chapters in Matthew: (1) Jews will be judged on the basis of their rejection of the Messiah (23:29-39), (2) Christians will be evaluated regarding their faith in Christ and their performance of assigned tasks (24:45-51, 25:14-30), (3) humans will be judged on the basis of good deeds and their avoidance of bad behavior (25:1-13).

Matthew's Last Judgment scene poses a major question of interpretation concerning the identification of "all the nations" who assemble before the Son of Man and his angels. Some experts believe that the evangelist is referring to all people, but others suggest from analysis of the Hebrew text that the Gentiles alone are present. Jewish and Christian apocalyptic writers often speak of two or more judgments, sometimes explicitly differentiating the judgment of Israel from that of the Gentiles. Many scholars thus see "all nations" as pagans who are neither Jewish proselytes nor converts to Christianity. Others maintain, on the other hand, that there is no separate standard for Jews and Gentiles; the judge separates as individuals, not as groups.

The other major question of interpretation is the identity of "one of the least of these who are members of my family." Some scholars point out that Jesus did identify himself with the poor, needy, and persecuted in Matthew 10:40-42 and Acts 9:4, 22:7, and 26:14. In a similar vein, exegetes claim that Jesus' solidarity with the poor is reflective of the Jewish *shaliach* principle: "a man's representative is as the man himself." What is distinctive in this passage in Matthew is the notion that all vulnerable people, even those with no conscious relationship with Christ, are nonetheless his representatives. In Matthew 25:31-46 this principle is extended to include all the world's powerless and needy.

A second school of thought is not as universal in its understanding of those identified with Jesus. Some Scripture experts believe that Jesus' self-identification with "least members of his family" does not extend in general to the poor and needy. To understand this passage as a basis for Christian love for the poor, indiscriminately considered, because the poor represent Christ, is reading into the text. These scholars suggest that for Matthew the term "brother" does not apply to all, but only to those who acknowledge Jesus as their Lord and Savior. Thus, for Matthew "brother" is a disciple or follower of Jesus. In this passage, therefore, "brothers" refers to members of the church. Some exegetes go as far as to limit Jesus' words to Christian missionaries, beginning with the apostles, who have been commissioned by Christ to preach his message in the world.

Interpretative questions also raise the issue of the passage's origins. Evidence, especially the pericope's startling originality, abounds that the passage is Matthean. The evangelist has prepared his readers with many earlier references to the coming of the Son of Man. Jesus' coming will be sudden and as conspicuous as lightning (24:27). He will be seen on the clouds of heaven and will send out his angels with a loud trumpet and gather the elect from the four winds (24:30f). The day and the hour of the Parousia are unknown; the world will be taken by surprise (24:36-42). The Last Judgment will be a day of reckoning (24:45-51) that may be delayed, but it will come nonetheless (24:48, 25:5, 19). Of all the evangelists only Matthew speaks of Christ's enthronement (19:28). He uses it in this Last Judgment passage to show Jesus as judge, as stated clearly in verse 31 and implied by the use of the term Lord as a title of address for the judge. The role of the Messiah as judge is almost without parallel in Judaism.

Another Matthean technique used in this passage is the principle of separation and judgment. In his Gospel the evangelist speaks of gathering wheat but burning chaff (3:12), separating weeds from wheat (13:30), angels separating the righteous from the wicked (13:49-50), five bridesmaids who enter and five who are locked out (25:12), and the lazy slave who buried his talent and is cast into the darkness (25:30). In separating sheep from goats Matthew is making yet another distinction between the elect and the damned.

Matthew also uses this pericope to express his Christology. In his Gospel the evangelist uses many titles for Christ — Son of Man (25:31), Messiah and Son of David (1:1—2:2, 21:4-9), Lord (25:37, 44), Messianic shepherd who cares for the sheep (2:6, 9:36, 18:12, 26:31), and judge who makes the final separation of the righteous and the evil (25:31). The many terms for Christ in this passage make it highly Christological. For Matthew it is this understanding of Jesus, and not a general humanitarianism, that validates the ethic of love and mercy that became the eschatological criterion for salvation.

The ultimate value of this passage is the concrete questions it raises in what criterion will be used at the Last Judgment. The answer appears to be that God will look for faith that has been lived in service to others. All the nations, however this is interpreted, will be examined concerning the acts of love which they have shown to Christ, who comes (again with different interpretations) in the form of the afflicted. Those who demonstrate such love will be granted the grace of a share in the Kingdom. One specific measure of this lived faith is the reception of Christian missionaries. Scholars suggest that Jesus is challenging all people to be open to his message as it will be promulgated by the apostles and their successors.

The end of Jesus' apocalyptic discourse raises a final question on Matthew's understanding of the Parousia. All indications are that Matthew expected the Second Coming in his lifetime. By the time his Gospel was composed a delay was already evident, meaning for him and others who believed similarly that the end was closer than ever. Matthew's conviction of the imminence of the Parousia is not speculative interest in calculating a time for the end, but rather is a pastoral concern. He wants Christians to be ready and to use their time wisely in the interim. Although writers have through the centuries devised many ways to try to rescue Matthew's misperception about the Parousia, it is more in accord with the nature of Scripture and the integrity to which the interpreter is called to allow Matthew to express his faith in apocalyptic terms, including its mistaken temporalities. Matthew will not be forced to become modern, but the contemporary reader can still be challenged by the apocalyptic message in all its urgency and compelling power.

Context Of The Parable

Context In The Church Year

The last Sunday of the liturgical year, known in many denominations as the Feast of Christ the King, closes the story of salvation history. The church has come full circle from Advent, which emphasized the Second Coming of Christ as well as preparation for the Lord's birth in history. Through the year the Christian community has walked with Jesus through his public ministry, stood by him as he trod the Via Dolorosa, and celebrated the resurrection with great fervor.

While Jesus is the high point of salvation history, its last chapter will be written at the Last Judgment, when all the nations will be assembled before the Lord and a separation will be made between the elect and the damned. It is appropriate, therefore, as the liturgical year closes that we hear the story of the final judgment and what criterion will be used by God to choose those who will inherit eternal life. The story of the sheep and goats forces us to pause in our busy lives, look inside, and ask, "Have I recognized Christ today?"

Context With The Other Gospels

While the synoptics and John make references to Jesus' return, this story of the sheep and goats is unique to Matthew. Sources of the story appear to be Mark (8:26f), as read and interpreted by Matthew in light of his concerns, Revelation, and the Hebrew Scriptures. The Q source does not seem to apply in this passage. The Book of Revelation (especially 20:11-15) is John the Evangelist's self-contained treatise on the Second Coming. In Ezekiel (34:17) the prophet speaks of God's separating Israel in groups — sheep and sheep, rams and goats. Old Testament references to God as king in an eschatological context (Isaiah 24:23, 33:22, Zephaniah 3:15, Obadiah 21, and Zechariah 14:16-17) lead scholars to believe this pericope may have some roots in Jewish literature. In Judaism the Messiah occasionally appears as King (Zechariah 9:9) and exercises God's sovereignty (Micah 5:1, 1 Chronicles 17:14). The apocryphal Book of Enoch's "The Epiphany of the Son of Man" (chapter 10, section 12) poses a similar scenario to Matthew's story.

Context With First And Second Lessons

First Lesson: Ezekiel 34:11-16, 20-24. The prophet Ezekiel presents two separate images of God as a shepherd. In the first half of this reading we hear an image similar to the Good Shepherd of John's Gospel. God will rescue those who have been scattered. The Hebrews in exile in Babylon at the time of Ezekiel's writing

181

would certainly have welcomed a message that spoke of how God would return the people to their land and give them rest. The prophet provides a message of hope in the midst of a sea of gloom. In the second half of this pericope we are presented with a more sobering message. God will rescue the people, but the Lord will also judge the nation of Israel. Those who have abused the weak will be punished for their actions. God will appoint one shepherd to pasture the sheep at the direction of God. This foreshadowing of the coming of Christ shows that the Messiah will be both savior and judge.

Second Lesson: Ephesians 1:15-23. Saint Paul tells the Ephesians that Christ is the head of the church and God the Father is the source of all wisdom. In the church all is subject to Christ, for the church is his body in all its universal parts. Christ is high above all principalities and dominations in this age or the age to come. It is the wisdom of God that will bring us insight to be able to know the Lord more fully and clearly.

Christ, the head of the church, challenges us to seek the wisdom of God that will place others before us. It is service, like that rendered by Paul, that will be the criterion upon which God will evaluate our lives. Following the lead of Christ in his public ministry will bring us home to eternal life with God.